The Kids' Catalog of
Animals and the Earth

Funding for this book is provided by the

Rebecca Meyerhoff Memorial Trust

in loving memory of

Rebecca Meyerhoff

Rebecca Meyerhoff's generosity, leadership,

and desire to promote literacy and Jewish education

have imparted an enduring legacy to the lives of

her children, grandchildren, and great-grandchildren.

May this book enrich the lives of its readers.

The Kids' Catalog of
Animals and the Earth

written and illustrated by
Chaya M. Burstein

The Jewish Publication Society
Philadelphia
2006 • 5766

Editor	Janet Greenstein Potter
Production Editor	Janet L. Liss
Production Manager	Robin Norman
Photo Research	JGPotter & Associates
Publishing Intern	Charlotte King
Design and Composition	Julia Prymak, Pryme Design

The Jewish Publication Society
2100 Arch Street
Philadelphia, PA 19103

Manufactured in the United States of America

06 07 08 09 10   10 9 8 7 6 5 4 3 2 1

Library of Congress Cataloging-in-Publication Data

Burstein, Chaya M.
　The kids' catalog of animals and the earth / written and illustrated by Chaya M. Burstein.— 1st ed.
　　p. cm.
　Includes index.
　ISBN 0-8276-0785-7 (alk. paper)
　1. Human ecology—Religious aspects—Judaism—Juvenile literature. 2. Environmental protection—Religious aspects—Judaism—Juvenile literature. 3. Animals—Religious aspects—Judaism—Juvenile literature. 4. Environmental law (Jewish law)—Juvenile literature. I. Title.
　BM538.H85B87 2005
　296.3'8—dc22

2005021718

To Betty—
who has known our Earth from the time of the horse and wagon until the 500-seat jet plane of today and is still optimistic about what comes next.

ACKNOWLEDGMENTS

So many people contributed to this book. Marilyn Whitford, Eden Trenor, Yossi Leshem, Bernard Goobich, and David Fine, among others, brought ideas and photos. Shulamit Wittenoff, Sim Goobich, Yoel Shechter, and Mike Gross made clear, constructive comments, as did my editors, Ellen Frankel, Carol Hupping, Janet Liss, and Janet Greenstein Potter. Many thanks to all of you. And to Mordy, who provided a steady supply of coffee, chocolate, and encouragement to keep me going.

Contents

Introduction

Imagine that two friends have the great, good luck of being able to talk to the earth, face to face. It's not exactly fun because the earth complains loudly about the way humans are messing up the natural environment. This gives the boy and girl (and us, the readers) some serious problems to think about. Actually, as the earth tells it, the problems aren't just serious, they're more like crucial—like matters of life and death. So we'd better look for answers, and fast!

First we'll find some good ideas about caring for the earth and its creatures in Jewish traditions and writings throughout history. Then we can go on to look at the problems carefully and try to decide whether they're really crucial or whether the earth is being kvetchy and making too big a deal about a little garbage and water pollution. But, if worse comes to worst, and we find that our Earth is really in terrible shape, we'll search for actions and activities to improve things—with the guidance of Jewish teachings, the advice of environmentalists, and a dash of your own great ideas.

Come join the conversation between the boy, the girl, and Mr/Ms Earth, and we'll hunt for answers together!

1 WE MEET THE EARTH

HEY YOU!!

WHO? US?

YEAH YOU! DO YOU REALIZE YOU'RE STANDING ON ME?

WE'RE STANDING ON THE EARTH.

THAT'S ME! I'M THE EARTH AND I WANT RESPECT! PICK UP THAT ICE CREAM WRAPPER.

OKAY. WHATEVER YOU SAY

I HAVE A LOT TO SAY. I'LL HOLOGRAM DOWN TO KID-SIZE SO I CAN LOOK YOU GUYS IN THE EYE WHEN I'M TALKING TO YOU.

WHOOSH

WHOOSH

W-WHAT'S HAPPENING?

IT'S HOLOGRAMMING

EEEE

SSSHHH

POP!

4

2 Starting with Creation

This page: Photo by Dr. James P. McVey,
Courtesy of NOAA Sea Grant Program.
Opposite page: Photo by Chaya M. Burstein.

In the Beginning

The first book of Jewish law, the Bible, describes the earth's beginnings very differently from the descriptions given by modern scientists. (More about that in chapters 6 and 7.) Right now, let's follow the story as the Bible tells it, to learn how the Jewish people valued and cared about the earth and its living things from the beginning.

Creating the earth and all its kinds of life was a very tricky matter. At first God had to work out a balance of air, land, and water to provide homes for living things. There was sun to warm and light the earth and to help make food for plants, and there was atmosphere and clouds to provide air to breathe and protect everyone from too much sun. When God got around to making living creatures, God had to balance their strengths so the strong ones didn't gobble up all the weak ones. And there had to be enough plants and water for everyone. A million things had to be juggled, to work out a balance between the earth and its tenants. Last of all, God made human beings. According to the Talmud (a book of law based on the Bible), God gave humans special instructions.

In the hour when the Holy One created the first human, God let the human pass before all the trees of the Garden of Eden and said, "All this I have created for

What could the Garden of Eden have looked like? The lush greenery of a waterfall in Hawaii? The fertile hills around the Sea of Galilee in Israel? We imagine it as a beautiful, fruitful, peaceful place—paradise. The Bible tells us only that streams flowed through the garden and that trees, plants, birds and animals of all kinds lived in it together.

DID YOU KNOW?

The Hebrew word for the entire Bible is TANAKH. The Bible has three sections, and Torah is the Hebrew name for the first section —also known as the Five Books of Moses. That's where the story of Creation is found.

you. Think about it and don't corrupt or ruin My world, because if you ruin it, there is no one to set it right after you."

God placed human beings in a green, fruitful garden called Eden, and told them to "till it and tend it." That was a big responsibility. People could use the earth to grow their food, but they had to take care of the earth as well. God also said, "Be fruitful and multiply. Fill the earth and master it." Being fruitful—having a lot of babies—made sense as well, because, according to the Bible, there was a human population of exactly two: Adam and Eve.

By the end of six days of Creation, God was ready to stop work, relax, and feel free. So the seventh day of the week became a day of rest, a *Shabbat*, the Hebrew word for Sabbath. God was satisfied with the work and said, "This is very good." Human beings stopped digging and poking and scrounging around for food. All creatures left each other in peace and rested. And the earth rested, too.

But almost immediately human beings began to mess around with the system.

First of all, Adam and Eve ate the fruit of the only tree that God had forbidden to them, so they were thrown out of the garden. Then Adam and Eve's son Cain committed the world's first murder. As soon as more people were born and grew up, they started killing and robbing each other. God got disgusted with all the murdering, fighting, and stealing, and God caused a great flood that drowned almost all living things. Only Noah, his family, and pairs of all other creatures were saved.

Some time afterward, Abraham became the first patriarch, or father, of the people of Israel. Although other people are important in the Bible's stories, most of its teachings are explained through the experiences of the Jewish people. There are stories of wars, heroism, and commandments, and of the Jewish people's powerful love of God and of Israel. But we won't tell those stories yet. We'll just tell about the small, important part of the Bible and other Jewish writings that relate to the earth and the natural environment—the animals, birds, oceans, rivers, fish, air, trees, and bugs.

Out of the Desert

The early Jewish people—the Israelites—had a special reason to love their land. They never took it for granted. As the Bible tells us, God called on Abraham to move his family to the Land of Israel, and he did. Later they left Israel and settled in fertile Goshen, in Egypt. Many years afterward, the Egyptians forced them to become slaves. It was only after a hard struggle that God and the Israelites' leader, Moses, brought the Jews out of slavery and into the desert. For the next 40 years they wandered through the grim, rocky wilderness on their way back to the Land of Israel. They were thirsty and tired and bored and scared.

People died, babies were born, and they were still stuck in the desert. When the tired Israelites finally reached the Jordan River and looked across at the land God had promised them, they couldn't believe their eyes. It was beautiful! Green, fertile, and filled with springs and streams of water. It was a land of milk and honey. Here's how the Bible describes it:

> *The Lord, your God, is bringing you*
> *into a good land, a land with streams and*
> *springs and fountains flowing from plain and*
> *hill, a land of wheat and barley, of vines, figs,*
> *and pomegranates, a land*
> *of olive trees and honey . . .*

(Deuteronomy 8:7–8)

After that they could never take the Land of Israel for granted. Every holiday became a celebration of their love of the land and a thank-you to God for bringing them out of the desert.

In earliest spring in Israel, when frost still silvers the fields and rain pours day after day, the almond tree bursts into bloom. Pink and white blossoms sparkle against the clouds. (Photo by Rivka Dorfman)

Passover in early spring celebrated the ripening of the first crop of grain—the barley. It was also a celebration of freedom from slavery in Egypt. The Israelites brought gifts of grain and animals to the Temple they had built for God in Jerusalem. And they danced and feasted and thanked God for providing the fruits of the earth. During the holiday, a book of the Bible called The Song of Songs is read. It tells about a springtime of flowers, new buds on fruit trees, and singing birds. A young man and woman run happily through the fields, in love with each other and with their land:

Natural Holidays

My beloved spoke thus to me,
Arise my darling;
My fair one, come away!
For now the winter is past,
The rains are over and gone.
The blossoms have appeared in the land,
The time of pruning has come;
The song of the turtledove
Is heard in our land.
The green figs form on
    the fig tree,
The vines in blossom
    give off fragrance.
Arise, my darling;
My fair one, come away!

(The Song of Songs 2:10–13)

DEFINITION, PLEASE!

A **sukkah** (plural **sukkot**) is a small hut or booth built for the holiday of Sukkot. It reminds us of the structures Jewish farmers once made, using branches and leaves, so they could sleep in the fields while bringing in the harvest.

DID YOU KNOW?

Some families today build a sukkah in their own backyard or on their balcony. To create the walls, people often use fabric on a frame. The stars of the sky should be visible through an open roof, ideally made of branches. Children like to decorate the sukkah with hanging fruits and vegetables, flowers and gourds, and their own artwork. During Sukkot, it is traditional to eat meals (and even sleep) in the sukkah.

From Passover until the next holiday of Shavuot, the Israelites anxiously counted off 50 days called the Omer. Why were they anxious? Because if too much or too little rain fell, if the wind blew ferociously or the sun hid behind clouds, their crops might die. But if the Omer went well, there would be full baskets of wheat by Shavuot. Then the people would bake brown loaves of bread and bring them to the Temple, along with the first fruits and first calves and lambs born in the springtime.

Shavuot was a farmer's holiday and also celebrated God's giving the Torah to the Jewish people. So again, prayers of thanks, singing, dancing, and the music of flutes, drums, trumpets, and rattles. At Shavuot the Jews read the Book of Ruth, a Bible story set during the barley and wheat harvests when Ruth and Boaz meet and fall in love—another love story that relates to the earth.

Sukkot, the third harvest holiday, was the biggest of the year. It celebrated the great harvest of the orchards and the fields each fall. And it was also a time for remembering the hard, 40-year hike through the desert after the Israelites left Egypt. By Sukkot the huge storage jars were full of grain. Olives were picked and squeezed for oil or set to soak in spices and salt water. Dates, figs, plums, and grapes were laid out to dry in the sun, and other grapes bubbled in dark jars as they turned into wine. Soon the rains would come, and the farmers would settle down for the quieter work of winter. But first they had a big bash! Back to the Temple they went, carrying tied-together branches of willow, myrtle, and palm, and a bright yellow citron (the *lulav* and *etrog* in Hebrew). They built booths called sukkot to live in, and they spent a week praying, feasting, arranging marriages, and telling stories around the campfires.

Village children in modern Israel pile into a tractor-pulled wagon at Shavuot for a ride through the flower-filled, springtime fields. (Photo by Chaya M. Burstein)

Time-out for the Earth— Shabbat, Shemitah, and Yovel

Most Israelites were farmers and shepherds. That's full-time work. Plants keep growing, chickens keep laying eggs, and goats and cows need to be milked. But the Israelites would not give up their *Shabbat*—the day of rest that God had commanded. They took care of essential work like milking and feeding, and then everyone got a day off. The earth, the people, their guests, servants, slaves, and farm animals all rested on the seventh day of each week.

Every seventh year the Bible called for a whole year of *Shabbat* for the earth—the *shemitah* year—when crops wouldn't be planted or harvested. For 12 months the earth would store up water and grow its wild plants freely until, at the end of the resting time, it was fertile and ready for action again.

The most amazing rest time for the earth was supposed to happen every 50 years. During that 50th year—the Jubilee year—land that people had sold was to be returned to them. Since God said, "The land is Mine. You are only strangers living with Me" (Leviticus 25:23), people had to understand that they didn't really own the land—they were just being allowed to use it for a while. And the fields were to lie unplanted and

DID YOU KNOW?

The first recorded harvest of watermelons was nearly 5,000 years ago in Egypt, where the fruit was admired not only for its flavor, but also for its beauty. Today watermelons are grown in 96 countries. Japanese farmers have even developed cube-shaped watermelons that will fit more easily into cardboard shipping boxes and refrigerators without rolling around! To make it happen, farmers grow the melons inside glass cubes, and the fruit naturally assumes the same shape.

unplowed as they did during the *shemitah*. We don't know if the Israelites fully observed the Jubilee. But *Shabbat*, at the end of each week, was, and still is, the most important holiday of any year.

The Good Earth

The center of life for the early Israelites was the earth. With desert lands all around them, they knew how lucky they were to be living in the fruitful land of Israel. During the hot, dry summers they prayed for dew to dampen their fields. In winter they prayed for rain to fill their cisterns—the storage basins they had dug under, or near, their houses. And at holiday time they came to the Temple and thanked God for the gift of faith and for their good earth.

Modern Israel isn't exactly flowing with streams and springs. But pioneering engineers have tapped the Sea of Galilee (also called the "Kinneret") and underground sources to provide water for irrigation, even as far south as the Negev. Watermelons are 92-percent water, so for them, irrigation is especially good news. Sweet round slices of watermelon, cut into handy-to-eat triangles, are often paired with the salty taste of cheese. Helping to make these delicious, healthy treats possible, the men in this photo are at work in a field near the town of Jericho. (Courtesy of Israelimages.com)

ECO-ACTIVITY

A PAPER EARTH

The Land of Israel is at the center of the earth's surface, and Jerusalem is at the center of the Land of Israel—that's what Hebrew and Christian scholars believed many years ago. Maps drawn in the Middle Ages show Jerusalem in the center, surrounded by the continents of the world. Today we know that the earth isn't a flat surface with a middle, sides, and corners. But Jerusalem and Israel are still central to many of us.

Learn some facts about Mr/Ms Earth, make a model of him/her, and then locate Israel, Jerusalem, and important places like your home and country on the model.

First, some facts. The earth's surface is mostly ocean (70 percent). The rest is land, some of which is desert (4 percent) and some is rain forest (7 percent, but that percentage is dropping fast). As far as we know the earth is the only planet in the solar system that supports living things. That's because it's surrounded by an atmosphere that protects the surface from the burning heat of the sun and holds enough moisture and necessary gases to keep life going. Deep down at the center—the core—the earth is unbelievably hot. Luckily for all of us, the layers get cooler and cooler—until at the surface there's usually a comfortable average temperature for plants and animals to live.

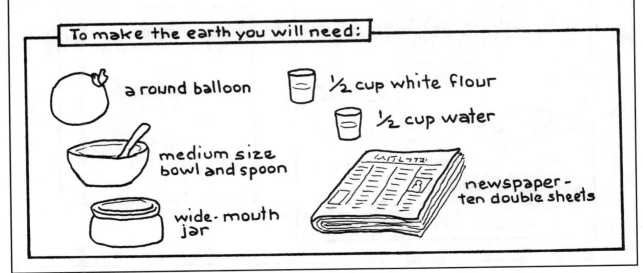

To make the earth you will need:

a round balloon

½ cup white flour

½ cup water

medium size bowl and spoon

wide-mouth jar

newspaper- ten double sheets

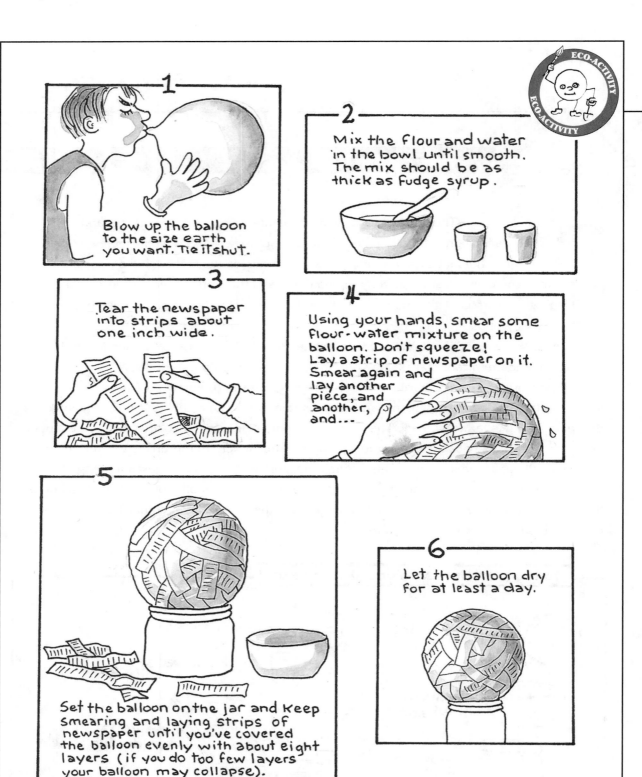

To paint the earth you will need:

world map

paints and brushes

pen or pencil

stiff paper such as poster board or index cards

tape

scissors

7

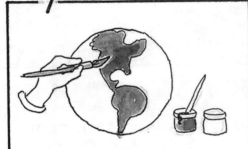

Look at the world map. Roughly draw the land on your model of the earth. Paint in the oceans and the land.

8

On the stiff paper draw and paint places and things that interest you — your home, trees, animals, the domes of Jerusalem, national flags, etc.
Cut them out, leaving tabs for taping.

tab

A LITTLE RESPECT PLEASE

SO HOW'M I DOING, MR/MS EARTH? SEE HOW MUCH WE JEWS APPRECIATE YOU?

NOT BAD. I LIKE THE STORY ABOUT HOW THE EARTH WAS CREATED. ALL THOSE PLANTS AND ANIMALS WORKING FOR EACH OTHER. AND THE SUN, OCEANS, CLOUDS, TREES. EVERYTHING KEEPING ME AND MY ATMOSPHERE IN BALANCE. NICE. VERY NICE.

DON'T FORGET HOW THE BIBLE HAS THESE LAWS ABOUT TAKING CARE OF THE EARTH.

YEAH, THE SHEMITAH YEAR IS GOOD. I NEED A REST EVERY FEW YEARS. AND I LIKE GOD'S IDEA THAT HUMANS DON'T OWN ME. THEY'RE LIKE GUESTS. YOU HUMANS CAN LIVE HERE ON EARTH BUT YOU MUST RESPECT ME AND NOT MESS ME UP.

'RESPECT' THAT'S MY MIDDLE NAME

BUT HOW ABOUT THE BIG STUFF? GARBAGE, PESTICIDES, KILLING OFF WHOLE SPECIES OF ANIMALS AND BIRDS?!

3 Birds, Animals, Pets, and Monsters

Living in Nature

In Bible times, people lived right in the middle of their natural environment. Goats, sheep, donkeys, and doves shared the front yards of their houses—and during the cold, rainy winters some families even invited the smaller animals and fowl in to help warm the house. Animals in Bible times may have lived on the floor in the center of the room while the people slept on a raised platform that ran along the walls. Wild pigs, bears, lions, foxes, and many more animals roamed in the woods around the villages. The pigs would crash through piles of firewood and manure, snuffling around for acorns and other things to eat. And the bears and lions would raid the flocks of sheep and goats, looking for juicy meals. Bible heroes like Samson and David made their ferocious reputations by killing lions and bears that threatened their flocks.

The Israelites knew their land well. Every cave, hill, large rock, plant, and animal had a name. People told stories about them around the fire on rainy, winter evenings, and while resting in the shade during the hot summers. When they walked the dirt roads between the villages, they felt and smelled their earth, because summer dust blew up and filled their noses, and winter mud squooshed between their toes. Before visitors were offered a cup of herbal tea, their hosts brought a basin of water and washed their feet, just as Abraham washed the feet of God's messengers in the Bible story.

Food came from the orchards and the fields, and it was all natural. No sprays, chemical fertilizers, or manipulated genes. Even the garbage was natural. Bright wrapping paper, insecticides, and plastic toys hadn't been invented yet. The garbage was biodegradable, which means it was easily broken down by insects and bacteria and absorbed by the earth. Only a few handmade things like clay pots, glass vases, stone or metal tools, and jewelry weren't absorbed. Today archaeologists love to dig up those leftovers and study them.

All that healthy, natural stuff sounds good, but it had its down side. No strawberries or peaches in January. No Chinese or Italian restaurants on Sunday evenings. Except for the rich, people ate very little meat. Only at holiday time, when they brought animal offerings to the Temple in Jerusalem, did they get to eat meat. On ordinary days the Israelites filled up on flat bread made of wheat that was freshly ground each morning, or on whatever fruits and vegetables were ready for picking. And there was usually cheese made from the milk of their sheep and goats.

It's breakfast time—but this Arab woman isn't making pancakes. She's grinding hard grains of wheat into flour for the morning pita bread. Using the same method as women did in the biblical era, she uses a stone bowl and pestle. (Photo by Rivka Dorfman)

Living with Animals

In the beginning, when all living things were in the Garden of Eden, humans didn't eat animals—and animals didn't eat humans, or even each other. According to the midrash (stories written by sages to explain the Torah), they were all peaceful vegetarians. But after the Great Flood, Noah and all the other creatures rushed off the ark and started hungrily gobbling each other up. Later, prophets like Isaiah were unhappy that people were killing and eating animals. Isaiah wrote of a gentle time in the future when all living things, even wild lions and bears, would stop killing each other.

The wolf shall dwell with the lamb,
The leopard shall lie down with the kid;
The calf, the young lion, and
*   the fat ox together.*
And a little child will lead them . . .
In all of My sacred mountain
Nothing evil or vile shall be done.

(Isaiah 11:6–7, 9)

In the meantime—even though people still ate animals, birds, fish, and certain insects—the Bible, the Talmud, and other Jewish law that followed demanded that all creatures be treated kindly. Jews were taught that they must feel the pain of living things—in Hebrew that's called *tzaar baalei chaim*—and must be careful not to hurt them unnecessarily. Here are a few reminders:

- Don't hitch an ox and a donkey together. (One is stronger than the other, and they won't be able to pull the plow evenly.)

- Don't muzzle the ox as it works to crush the grain. (The animal has a right to eat some grain while it works.)

- It is forbidden for you to eat before you have fed your animal.

- On Shabbat, your work animal should rest just as you rest. And let it run free in the field on its day of rest.

- If your enemy's donkey falls down under its heavy load, you must help raise it up. (Even if you don't want to help your enemy, out of pity you must help the animal.)

- When you take eggs out of a bird's nest, you must first drive away the mother bird. Watching the eggs be removed

DEFINITION, PLEASE!

The **Talmud** is a book of Jewish law and lore containing explanations and interpretations of the Bible's teachings. It was written by many generations of Jewish scholars and rabbis, mostly in an ancient language called Aramaic, and has more than 2½ million words.

would cause her grief and distress. (If she doesn't see what happened, she will later lay more eggs, and the species will not die out.)

- Don't hunt animals just for sport. That's called "wanton bloodshed."

- Staging animal fights for entertainment is forbidden. Don't even attend a bullfight.

- Don't rejoice about something that causes suffering to an animal. For instance, don't say *tet-hadesh* (the greeting used when someone is wearing new clothing) when a person is wearing new leather shoes or a new fur coat, because this clothing cost an animal its life.

Living with Pets

We don't mow the lawn with oxen or ride to school on donkeys today. For most of us, work animals aren't part of our lives anymore. But we do have pet animals. Cats, dogs, hamsters, and parakeets are like family members. So think about the reminders from the Bible and Talmud. Stretch them a little and see how they apply to you and your pets. For example:

- Don't forget to feed your pet at a regular time each day.

- Even if you're busy, make time to take your dog to a park or open field where it can run or roam freely.

- Play with your pets. They need your love and attention.

- Be kind to your neighbor's animal and to a stray as well as to your own pet.

- Make sure your pet gets shots and other care by a vet when needed.

- Be sure to clean your pet's cage or litter box regularly.

- If you don't want or can't keep your pet anymore, don't drop it off in the middle of nowhere and abandon it. Rather, take it to an animal shelter or, better yet, find it a loving new home.

It's been a long, wonderful day of riding. Hannah is sure to feed Merlin his grain before sitting down to her own meal. (Photo by Bill Buckley. Courtesy of Epona Equine)

PET QUESTIONS

You may love your pet as much as you love your brother or sister. Sometimes maybe more! Your pet may be your best friend, your responsibility, and your playmate. Because pets are so important, questions come up that are hard to answer. What if your pet gets very sick? Would you have it euthanized—"put it to sleep"? Would you say *Kaddish*, a memorial prayer, after a pet died? Would it make sense for a rabbi to bless a pet? What if your pet had a litter of kittens or puppies that nobody wanted? What would you do? There's a lot to think about. To solve these kinds of pet problems, look in chapter 8 for ideas that grow out of Jewish traditions.

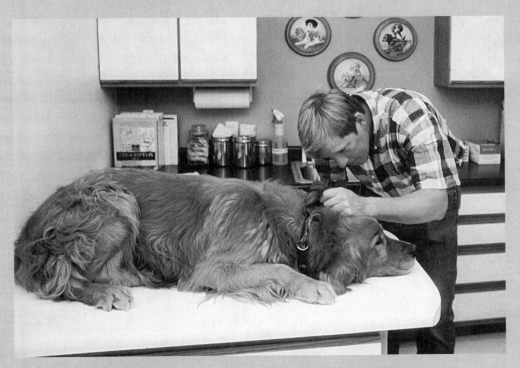

Griz is a good patient. This golden retriever is at the vet for his annual vaccinations and checkup. Now do those ears need cleaning? (Courtesy of thegreenagency.com)

Animals in the Land of Israel

The Bible and the Talmud tell many stories about animals and birds. There are wild animals, tame ones, ferocious and cuddly ones, and even imaginary ones. Here are some that we read about most.

LIONS

Lions are mentioned more than 150 times in the Bible. The very strong man called Samson tore a lion apart with his hands. And when King David was a shepherd boy, he grabbed a lion by the mane and hit it with a club after it stole a lamb from his flock. Daniel, thrown into a den of lions, gave bellyaches to the big cats when an angel prevented them from eating him up. Even though lions in the Bible sometimes had humiliating experiences and even though these animals have been extinct in Israel for a thousand years, the "Lion of Judah" is still a symbol of strength and glory in Jewish art. It decorates Torah arks and Torah curtains in countless synagogues.

FOXES

Foxes still roam at night in the Galilee in northern Israel and in the Negev, a desert region in the south. King Solomon complained that they spoiled the grapevines, but foxes today don't bother very much with grapes. They prefer mice and other small rodents.

JACKALS

Jackals are described as large foxes in the Bible. When Samson was angry at the Philistines, because his Philistine girlfriend married someone else he used jackals for revenge. He attached flaming sticks to their tails and sent hundreds of jackals to burn the Philistines' fields. The nighttime howling of jackals keeps Israelis awake in modern times just as it did in Bible times. Jackals were, and are, the garbage cleaners of the land—they eat dead animals.

BROWN BEARS

Brown bears once lived in the forests of Israel. David, the brave shepherd, fought off a bear. But bears disappeared a hundred years ago as the forests were chopped down.

BOARS

A boar isn't a cute, plump, pinkish farm pig. It's a wild pig with a bristly, black coat, a straight tail, and sharp tusks. Boars once lived in the marshes near the Jordan River. Today they've moved up into the Galilee mountains, where at night, families of boars root around in gardens and orchards. They dig up tubers (underground stems) and hunt for rodents.

CAMELS

The groaning, complaining camel has been the "ship of the desert" since Bible times. Maybe earlier. It plods along, fully loaded with 400 to 600 pounds of goods at about three miles an hour, swaying from side to side like a ship in rough seas. Camels have broad feet with toes that spread and help them walk on sand. They have large stomachs and can drink gallons of water, which is absorbed by their bodies and used on dry days in the desert. And the hump on the camel's back is almost all fat, which gives it energy when food is scarce. Biblical Rebecca won herself a husband (Isaac) when she generously hauled water from the well for Eliezer, Abraham's servant, and his 10 thirsty camels.

IBEXES

Sharp-eyed, black-bearded, and sure-footed were the wild goats—the ibexes—that lived in the rocky Judean hills above the Dead Sea. They've been hunted till they're almost extinct. Today they're protected in a wildlife sanctuary in the Negev.

A Delicate Balance

Herds of deer have quickly grown very large in many rural and suburban parts of the eastern United States because their natural enemies—the wolves, wildcats, and bears—are long gone. Now, hungry deer eat all the leaves off young trees growing in the woods, raid gardens, and follow railroad tracks in the winter to search for food that may have been dropped from the trains.

We are finally understanding that all creatures, even wolves, have a place in nature's eco-system. When a species is eliminated, the balance of living things is affected. Israeli naturalists have brought pairs of wolves back to the Golan Heights, and in the United States wolves are once again roaming freely in Yellowstone Park.

Sometimes there's trouble when people introduce new, non-native species to an area. For example, the mongoose was brought to the Virgin Islands to eat snakes and ended up eating everything in sight. Rabbits were brought to Australia to serve as food, but with no natural enemies they speedily multiplied and took over. Rabbits and mongeese . . . everywhere!

DEER

Several kinds of deer lived in the forests of Israel. Isaac, one of the biblical forefathers, asked his older son Esau, a hunter, to bring him a dish of tasty venison (deer meat). Isaac promised that after his meal he would bless Esau with the once-in-a-lifetime blessing of the firstborn. But the venison arrived too late (Esau's disguised brother Jacob sneaked in earlier with a delicious dish for their nearly blind father), and Esau lost out on his blessing. Of course, the deer wasn't to blame, but it lost out, too, because later, as the forests of Israel disappeared, so did the deer. Today deer are being raised in preserves and slowly being set free into the woods.

WOLVES

The Bible describes the tribe of Benjamin as a hungry wolf, which devours his enemy in the morning. This phrase means that members of the tribe were fearless, mighty warriors. Real wolves were hated in ancient Israel because they loved to eat sheep and lambs. Today only a few hundred wolves remain, protected by Israel's wildlife laws. They hunt gazelles, hares, rodents, wild pigs, and ibexes, but they also sometimes raid people's garbage or prey on farmers' livestock.

ONAGERS

Though it's related to the patient, plodding donkey, the onager is a fast, wild ass which once lived in the desert as far away from people as possible. Its coloring depends on the season—reddish brown in the summer and yellowish brown in the winter, with a black stripe bordered in white down its back. Thousands of years ago, people in Mesopotamia captured onagers to be used for pulling chariots, but most were too swift and strong to be caught. Because of modern hunting and loss of grazing habitat, there are no onagers left in the wild today. Israel and Jordan are breeding them in nature preserves to try to keep the species alive.

STRIPED HYENAS

Striped hyenas prowled at night in ancient Israel. They were a clean-up crew like the jackals, eating garbage, dead animals, and even the bodies of people killed in battle. In Bible times, the prophet Jeremiah scolded rich Israelites for oppressing the strangers among them and the poor widows and orphans. He cried out that God sees the people of Israel behaving like hyenas or like birds of prey.

LEOPARDS

Smaller than a lion or a tiger but just as deadly a hunter, the leopard crouches on a tree branch over a trail, ready to drop onto the back of a passing deer or antelope. In the Bible, Jeremiah predicted disaster for the Israelites who broke God's laws by saying, "A leopard will watch over their cities and everyone who goes out will be torn to pieces."

There are very few leopards left in Israel, but a smaller cat called the caracal still roams the Negev.

DOGS

There were no fancy poodles, spaniels, or boxers in ancient Israel. There was only one breed of dog—it was tan, short-haired, slinking, and savage. The Israelites didn't like dogs. Again and again the Bible compared an undesirable person to a dead dog. It was many years before dogs were accepted and fed and became guards, helpers, and friends to their owners.

Many other wild animals still roam through Israel's hills and deserts. Porcupines bumble along paths in the north. Hyrax (rock rabbits) sunbathe on rocky ledges over the Dead Sea. And gawky ostriches gallop through nature preserves, poking their heads into tourists' car windows. If you're sitting in a meadow having a peaceful lunch, hold tight when a herd of goats ambles by. They're domesticated, for sure, but they're wild about peanut-butter sandwiches.

Domestic animals move through all the Bible stories. Each day they worked hard beside their human owners, and many of them were brought to the Temple as offerings to God. Patient donkeys carried heavy loads. Goats and sheep

Camels once had many purposes in desert life. Besides transporting their masters, who liked to ride them and race them, camels transported heavy loads of goods on their backs. Bedouins (the wandering tribes of the North African and Middle Eastern deserts) drank camel's milk, used camel's hair to weave tent fabric, and ate camel meat. Camels are still occasionally seen at work in parts of Saudi Arabia, Jordan, and in desert areas of other Middle Eastern countries. This Bedouin boy and girl are keeping an eye on the family's camel at their camp beside the Dead Sea. (Photo by Ed Toben)

provided wool, milk, cheese, meat, and leather. Oxen, water buffalo, and sometimes camels pulled ploughs and wagons. Some of these animals are still around, still working, but not for long. Tractors, trucks, and cars are taking over their jobs.

A SAFE HAVEN

Over the millions of years that living creatures have been on Earth, countless species have been born, lived, and died, or became extinct. We all know about the dinosaurs that roamed the earth until 65 million years ago and left us only their fossilized bones. But since we humans have spread across the planet and changed the natural environment, species of animals have begun to disappear more quickly than ever before. Endangered animals are often placed in protected areas called preserves. There they can safely "be fruitful and multiply." Chimpanzees live successfully in the jungle of the Gombe preserve in Tanzania; oryx, addax, caracal, and onagers live in preserves in Jordan and Israel; bison (buffalo) live in preserves in some central and western parts of the United States. And there are many more protected areas all over the world.

An addax is a typical desert dweller with large, spreading hoofs for walking on soft sand. It goes most of its life without drinking and gets all the moisture it needs from dew or from its diet of coarse grasses and succulent plants. A kind of antelope, its ancestors once roamed in large numbers from the Atlantic Ocean to the Nile River. But since the 1800s, its numbers have been shrinking. Grazing peacefully, this addax does not realize it's nearly the last of its species. It lives in a preserve where naturalists hope it will find a mate with which to be fruitful and multiply. (Photo by Mary Clay. Courtesy of ardea.com)

Birds Are Tourists and Residents

Though Israel is a small country, it's a land bridge between Europe and the warmer lands of Asia and Africa. Each spring for countless centuries flocks of storks, cranes, swallows, quail, and other birds have flown north over Israel to enjoy the summer in Europe. And in the fall they hurry back south, leaving Europe's cold winter for Africa's sun and warmth. Once, God sent migrating quail to fill the bellies of complaining Israelites when they were wandering in the desert.

Today bird lovers with cameras and binoculars rush to the Jordan Valley or the Aravah Valley to watch the flocks fly over. The birds wheel and swirl in great curves, turning from snow white to dark gray as the sun catches their backs and then their undersides. Among the birds that fly over are yellow wagtails, short-toed larks, shrikes,

About 500 million migrating birds cross Israel's narrow air space twice every year. These storks are coming down to rest in the Hula Valley, halfway on their spring trek from Europe to Africa. (Courtesy of Israel Nature Reserves Authority)

bluethroats, and honey buzzards. These brave migrations over thousands of miles make us marvel, but they also cause problems, as you will see in chapter 10.

Other birds aren't just tourists—they *live* in Israel. There are doves whose ancestors were brought to the Temple in Jerusalem as gifts to God, and others who announce the coming of spring. As The Song of Songs tells, "The voice of the turtledove is heard in the land." Doves are still raised for food in dovecotes in Arab villages. Crows caw loudly from phone wires, and eagles hunt small animals along the jagged slopes of Israel's mountains. At the seashore, long-legged herons, ibises, and egrets hunt for food. Hoopoes are Israel's flashiest birds, with a crown of cinnamon feathers and black-and-white-striped wing and tail feathers. And there are hawks, owls, pelicans, partridges, and more.

DID YOU KNOW?

In the Western Hemisphere, many birds and butterflies spend the winter in the Caribbean, Mexico, or Central America—and some go as far as South America. As that season ends, they migrate north to follow the sun and to lay their eggs in regions with fewer predators. When you hear the sweet solo of a warbler or a thrush in your backyard, you'll know for sure that it's spring and the wanderers have come back to nest.

An eagle is floating on the air currents above Gamla—a mountain in the Golan Heights that resembles a camel's hump. This bird is a raptor—he hunts, kills, and eats meat using his keen eyesight, sharp talons, and hooked beak. He looks relaxed and lazy, but, down below, the plump rock rabbits and mice aren't fooled. They dash wildly to their holes when they see him. (Photo by Dov Goobich)

Plain old, ordinary animals like lions and bears weren't enough for our ancestors. In the Bible and Talmud, people told stories of amazing, imaginary, powerful creatures that terrified all other living things and gave the kids nightmares.

Monsters and Fantastic Creatures

SHAMIR

The smallest creature was the shamir—a worm no bigger than a grain of barley but strong enough to split gigantic mountains. The hoopoe, which guarded the tiny shamir, would fly over desolate mountains holding the shamir in its beak. It would drop the tough, little worm onto a bare mountain, where the shamir cut a crevice in which plants and trees could grow. The shamir's hardest job was to help build the great Temple in Jerusalem. Since no metal could be used to cut stone for the House of God, the shamir stretched out on the stone and cut it into building blocks. When the work was done, the tired little worm crawled deep into the Temple to rest. Years later, when the Temple was destroyed by Babylonian enemies, the shamir disappeared and hasn't been seen since.

ZIZ-SHADDAI

Is it a plane? Is it a rocket? It's *ziz-shaddai*, king of the birds! He's so big that his head brushes the top of the sky, and when he flies across the sun his wings turn day into night. God appointed this giant bird to protect us from the cold and storms of winter. He spreads his wings and shelters all of us beneath them.

PHOENIX

Another bird, the phoenix, was the only bird in the Garden of Eden who wouldn't eat the forbidden fruit. As a reward, it lives for 1,000 years and runs beneath the sun, spreading the sun's warmth with its great wings. With 1,000 years of running, the phoenix should qualify for the Olympic games, but its appearance might scare off the other runners—

DEFINITION, PLEASE!

A **legend** is a story that comes down to us from the past, and both the storyteller and the listeners believe the story could possibly be true. They just can't prove it.

it has a crocodile's head, a lion's feet and tail, and bright purple feathers. Every thousand years the phoenix lays an egg and dies, and a baby bird hatches and immediately starts running. In another version of the phoenix legend, the bird burns up and then renews itself from its ashes.

BEHEMOTH

A peaceful, plant-eating monster, so big that it swallows the water of the Jordan with one gulp, is the behemoth. With a tail as thick as a cedar tree and bones like brass, it could do lots of damage. But it's too lazy or mild-mannered to hurt anyone, except in midsummer. Then it rears up on its hind legs and roars a warning to wild animals not to attack domestic animals—or else!

LEVIATHAN

There's nothing mild-mannered about the leviathan. Sparks and flames shoot from its mouth and smoke pours from its nostrils. Some say it has several heads—which makes for a lot of smoke and flames. The leviathan is a monster that rules over fish. If you believe in legends, watch out for the leviathan when you're out kayaking. Paddle away from fire, smoke, and a boiling sea as fast as you can!

There are also the *re-em* (a gigantic fierce, fast, horned animal), the dragon, the *keresh* (a large, rainbow-colored unicorn), and more. Bows and arrows, slingshots—nothing can harm them. But, some of

ANIMAL SAYINGS FROM JEWISH LORE

- Don't put the cat in charge of the cream.
- Better to be a live dog than a dead lion.
- Better to be a tail to a lion than a head to a fox.
- The milk of a black goat and a white goat tastes the same.
- Drive your horse with oats, not with a whip.
- When an ox falls, many people sharpen their knives.
- If a wolf comes to kill you, you are not bound to pat his back.
- The wagon rests in winter. The sleigh rests in summer. The horse—never.

them come to a violent end. Legends tell that when the Messiah comes, at the end of time, the behemoth and the leviathan will have a gargantuan, roaring, thumping battle in which they'll kill each other. Then all good people will feast on a *ziz-shaddai*–behemoth–leviathan stew. Vegetarians, please stay home.

ECO-ACTIVITY

FEED THE BIRDS

In the winter birds need fatty foods to stay warm.

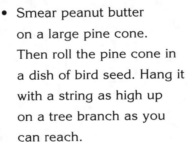

- Smear peanut butter on a large pine cone. Then roll the pine cone in a dish of bird seed. Hang it with a string as high up on a tree branch as you can reach.

- Get suet (animal fat) from the butcher. Tie it to a string or put it in a mesh bag and hang it from a branch or wrap it around a tree trunk as high as you can.

Once you start putting food out, birds begin to depend on it, so be sure to keep putting it out, especially in the winter.

40

GETTING EXTINCT

ALL RIGHT ALREADY. I GOT THE PICTURE. YOU JEWS USED TO LIVE IN A FRUITFUL, GREEN LAND WITH LOTS OF WILD AND TAME ANIMALS.

AND OUR BIBLE AND TALMUD GAVE US GOOD RULES ABOUT HOW TO TAKE CARE OF THE EARTH AND THE ANIMALS.

YOU SURE HAD SOME WEIRD ONES. I HOPE ZIZ-SHADDAI AND HIS FRIENDS AREN'T AROUND ANY MORE. BUT YOUR CROCODILES AND LIONS ARE GONE TOO. AND DEER AND ONAGER LIVE IN PRESERVES.

THAT'S FOR THEIR OWN GOOD. THEY'D DIE IF WE LET THEM RUN LOOSE.

THAT'S DISGUSTING! YOU'RE SPOILING THE WHOLE BALANCE OF MY WORLD IF LIVING CREATURES CAN'T RUN FREE.

ACCORDING TO THE MASTER PLAN, SOME OF THEM EAT GRASS, AND SOME OF THEM EAT THE GRASS-EATERS. IF IT GETS TOO CROWDED OR THEY RUN OUT OF FOOD A FEW MILLION DIE OFF AND WE'RE BACK IN BALANCE.

Living with Plants, Trees, and Other Green Things

Pluses and Minuses

Life wasn't all peaches and cream (or grapes and olives) for the farmers of Israel. Even though they lived in a land of milk and honey, there were problems. First, of course, there were human enemies. But let's save them for the next chapter. Second, there were natural problems like not enough rain, or too much rain, or a plant-shriveling *hamsin* (a hot, dry wind from the desert), or pounding hailstorms, or invasions of hungry locusts that devoured every leaf. In spite of these problems, the farmers of Israel and of the fertile lands to the north and south are thought to be the first farmers in the world. About 10,000 years ago they began to grow the first cereal crops (so blame your breakfast oatmeal on them). The seeds of fat ears of Middle Eastern wheat spread quickly to Europe and Asia.

Seven Species and More

Many plants and trees grew in this crescent of fertile lands on the eastern shore of the Mediterranean Sea. When the Hebrew tribes were still in the desert, God described seven species of plants they'd find in the Promised Land. There would be barley, wheat, grapes, figs, pomegranates, olives, and honey (made from dates, not by bees). There were also broad beans, lentils, and chickpeas that grew on bushy plants. Children in Israel would sit around toasting pods of chickpeas just as we toast marshmallows or make popcorn today. And a pot of simmering lentils caused the Bible's Esau to lose his birthright to his younger brother, Jacob. Esau was starving when he came home from hunting one day. He begged Jacob for a bowl of his delicious soup. "If you'll give me your right to inherit Papa's blessing and his property, I'll give you a bowl of soup," said Jacob. "Done!" Esau replied.

Flax grew in the hottest part of the country—the Jordan Valley. Its fibers were used to make linen cloth, and fishing lines and nets. During Bible times cotton wasn't yet used for cloth—and nylon, polyester, and rayon hadn't been invented. So in the summer, rich people enjoyed cool linen, which was expensive, and everyone else had to use smelly fur hides, or scratchy clothing made of goat's hair or camel's hair or sheep's wool.

Garlic, onions, almonds, leeks, and melons added spice to the daily diet. And olives, figs, grapes, and dates were used all year round—fresh, pickled, squeezed, fermented, and any other way people could concoct.

Dos and Don'ts

Most Jews were farmers when the Bible and the Talmud were written, so those books have a lot to say about caring for the earth and its green plants. In the Garden of Eden, the first humans were told that they could work the land but they must also take care of it. The Talmud warns, "You should learn that without land there is no rain, without rain there's no land, and without both of them there are no people." Here's some more advice from the sages:

- Don't throw rocks into a well from which you've drunk. (The water must stay clean to serve you and others.)

- Don't raise small animals such as sheep or goats near the woods and don't chop down good trees. (Sheep and goats eat vegetation right down to the roots and kill the trees. Even worse, when the tree roots die, the earth around them washes away.)

- A city must have a large green space around it. And that space may not be built upon. It must remain green for future generations. Rashi and Maimonides, two great Jewish sages of the 11th and 12th centuries, based this modern-sounding advice on the Torah. The Torah commanded that land must be set aside to build cities for the tribe of Levi, which did not receive a portion of land as the other tribes did. Those cities would be surrounded by open spaces and would belong to the Levites forever.

- Even during a war you must respect growing things. "If you are besieging a city you must not chop down the surrounding fruit trees," says the Bible. Trees are not humans—they can't withdraw inside the walls of a city before the enemy arrives. You may eat their fruit, but you may not destroy them. *Bal tash'hit*—don't destroy! Scholars and teachers have broadened the concept of *bal tash'hit* over the centuries. (More about this in chapter 11.)

In the days of the Bible, the hills of Israel were covered with forests. But for many centuries after that time, armies from different nations marched back and forth across the small land. War followed war, and each invading army used the trees and farms of the land ruthlessly.

The final blow to the country's forests was struck by the occupying Turks, who used the trees to make railroad ties and to build fortifications. In spite of intensive tree planting by the Jewish National Fund and the State of Israel, many hillsides like this one in northern Israel remain bare and eroded. (Photo by Chaya M. Burstein)

- If you're planting a tree and the Messiah comes, first finish planting and then go to greet the Messiah. The Messiah is God's messenger who will bring peace and happiness to the world. Only the planting of trees and caring for the earth could be more important than the Messiah.

- Don't take any of the earth's gifts for granted. Say a special blessing—a thank-you to God—before eating any food.

Our ancestors gave us good advice. Don't dirty the water. Leave green space. Don't destroy any part of the natural world without a very good reason. Planting and helping things to grow is more important than almost anything else. And be grateful for our generous Earth and the good food it provides.

The Trees' New Year—Tu b'Shevat

The tax collector and his donkey would come clip-clopping up to Israelite farms about the 15th day of the Hebrew month of Shevat. Any fruit tree he found that had blossomed before the 15th would be taxed for the previous year. If it had blossomed after the 15th, it would be taxed for the next year. The farmers surely didn't make a party for the tax collector. Who loves tax collectors? But many years later in the city of Safed in northern Israel, the trees' new year became a happy holiday—a day for leaving the stuffy study halls, walking on the hills, and breathing deeply. The people of Safed also celebrated by sitting together in a special seder—a ritual of tasting the fruits, nuts, and seeds of the land, blessing each one, and singing happily. Today, on Tu b'Shevat many Jews make a party for the earth and its trees and plants. An important (and delicious) part of the seder is tasting the nuts and fruits carefully and blessing each one, just as our Safed ancestors did.

Trees are the largest plants that inhabit the earth. Year after year, they continue to grow and provide people with necessities—such as fruits and nuts, lumber, pulp for paper, and, of course, sap for maple syrup. In fact, much of life on Earth owes its existence to trees. They shade and cool and shelter other living things. They provide homes for animals to live in and nest. They hold the soil in place to slow down the runoff of water. And even after trees die, as they decompose, they provide nutrients for the earth.

On Tu b'Shevat, the Jewish Earth Day, we're celebrating the earth and its complicated weave of millions of kinds of living things—including us—all dependent on air, water, and earth for survival. Tu b'Shevat is also a holiday to give thanks for the beauty and bounty of trees. Israelis put on boots and sweaters and go out in the forest to plant seedlings, which is what a baby tree is called. A teen-age tree is called a sapling. (Courtesy of Jewish National Fund)

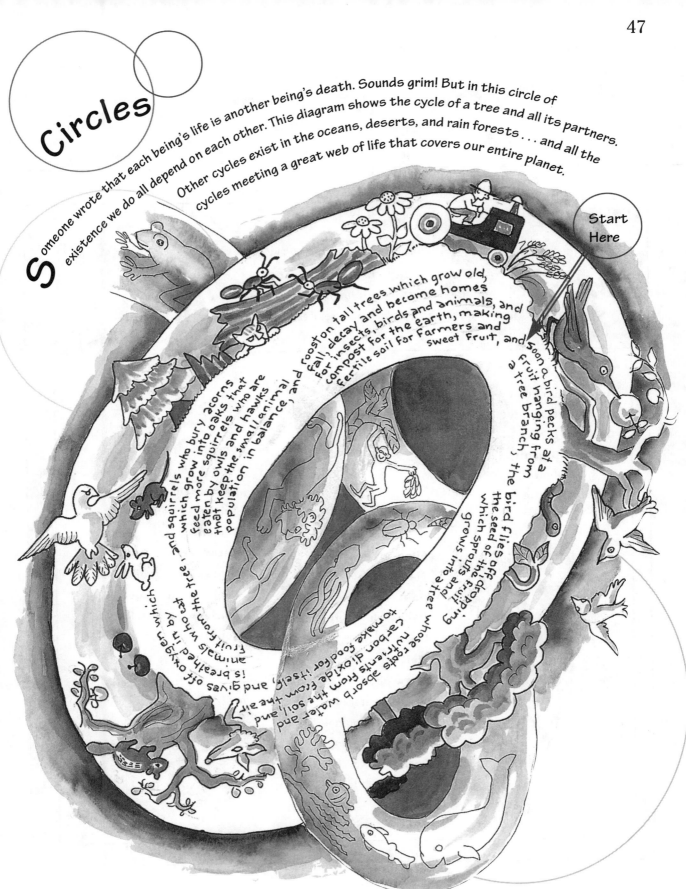

Circles

Someone wrote that each being's life is another being's death. Sounds grim! But in this circle of existence we do all depend on each other. This diagram shows the cycle of a tree and all its partners. Other cycles exist in the oceans, deserts, and rain forests . . . and all the cycles meeting a great web of life that covers our entire planet.

Start Here

. . . soon a bird pecks at a fruit hanging from a tree branch, the bird flies off which sprouts and grows into a tree whose roots absorb water and nutrients from the soil, and carbon dioxide from the air to make food for itself and gives off oxygen which is breathed in by animals who eat the tree and fruit from which feed more squirrels who are eaten by owls and hawks that keep the small animal population in balance, and rooston tall trees which grow old, fall, decay and become homes for insects, birds and animals, and compost for the earth, making fertile soil for farmers and sweet fruit, and . . .

. . . the seed of the dropping the bird flies off which sprouts and grows into a tree . . . acorns which grow into oaks that feed more squirrels and squirrels who bury acorns . . .

NATURAL NAMES

Once people searched the Bible for baby names. There were countless little Abrahams, Judiths, Esthers, and Jacobs toddling around. Bible names are still popular, but many Israeli parents like to choose names from nature, like these:

FOR GIRLS

Aviva   springtime
Ayala, Ayelet   doe
Devora   bee
D'ganya, D'ganit
      cornflower
Dikla   palm tree
Irit   iris

Eilah   terebinth tree
Elana   tree
Galit   ocean wave
Hadassah   myrtle bush
Leelach   lilac
Meital   water of dew
Nitza   bud
Nofar   water lily
Ofrah   young deer
Ora   light or brightness
Rachel   ewe, sheep
Shoshana   lily or rose

Smadar   bud, blossom
Talya   dew of God
Tzipporah   bird
Tamar   date palm
Tzviah   deer or gazelle
Vered, Varda   rose
Yaarah   forest or woods
Yael   mountain goat
Yardena   Jordan River
Yonat   dove

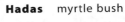

Hadas   myrtle bush
Jonah, Yonah   dove
Nir   furrow or plowed field
Ofer   young deer
Or   light or brightness
Oren   pine tree
Orev   raven
Rotem   broom bush
Shaked   almond tree
Tal   dew
Tomer   date palm
Tzvi   deer
Zev   wolf

For Boys

Alon   oak tree
Ari, Arieh   lion
Barak   lightning
Dov   bear
Dror   swallow (bird)
      or freedom
Ilan   tree

Eshel   tamarisk tree
Eyal   deer
Gad   coriander
Gal   ocean wave
Goor   cub
Gai   valley

GROWING THINGS

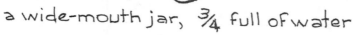

Make a miracle happen!

Watch a
bare branch grow flowers
in mid-winter—root a forsythia

At Tu b'Shevat, cut a bare forsythia
branch in your garden or buy a branch at the flower shop.
Put it in a jar of water, where it will form roots. Then watch it
bud, flower, and "leaf out" over the next few weeks. In early
spring plant the rooted branch in the garden.

Or, here's another idea—grow an avocado tree in a jar

You will need:

3 toothpicks

an avocado pit

a wide-mouth jar, ¾ full of water

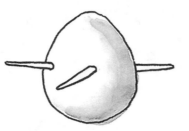

1

Stick the toothpicks
into the side of the pit,
at its middle.

2

Put the pit in the
jar with its
flatter end down,
and support it
with the tooth-
picks resting
on the top edge
of the jar.

ECO-ACTIVITY

If your avocado is too tough to pierce you will need:

a knife

a large paper cup (8-ounce size)

a wide-mouth jar 3/4 full of water

an avocado pit

1

Cut an 'X' in the bottom of the cup.

2

Hold the pit with the flatter end down and push it halfway through the 'X'.

Put the paper cup with the pit into the jar.

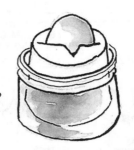

Add water every few days so that the bottom of the pit is always in water. Roots will grow from the pit, usually within three to five weeks. A few weeks after the roots start growing, the pit will split partway, and a leaf will push its way out and up. Then you can plant the seed in a flowerpot filled with potting soil. Keep it on a sunny windowsill and water it whenever the soil feels dry.

5 Stories with Roots

Centuries of Tales

Are you wondering why there's suddenly a chapter of stories? It's not only to keep Mr/Ms Earth calm. It's also because stories have always been used to teach and explain.

Instead of lecturing to people about the need to treat animals kindly, a rabbi would tell a story about Judah the Prince, who learned about kind treatment only after an eleven-year-long toothache. Other stories, like one about young Israel Ben Eliezer, and poems, like one by Rachel Bluestein, express our feeling of closeness to the trees and animals and natural world around us. Also, over the centuries, stories helped the Jews to stay connected to their lost homeland, the Land of Israel.

Up to this chapter, you've read about the connection that the Jewish people had to the earth as farmers and shepherds. But about 2,000 years ago the Land of Israel was conquered by the Roman Empire. The Temple in Jerusalem, the heart of Jewish culture and religion, was destroyed, and the Jews were forced to leave their land.

Centuries passed. Jews became craftsmen and merchants and lived in cities far from their homeland. How could they bring harvest gifts to God in the Temple if their holy Temple was just a pile of blackened stones? How could they love the earth and celebrate their holidays when they had been torn away from their fields and orchards? They would not give up and they would not forget! They began to study their holy books and pray to God in synagogues, instead of bringing sacrifices to the Temple. And they added historic meaning to the old harvest holidays. Passover meant escape from slavery to freedom; Shavuot celebrated God's gift of the Torah; and Sukkot reminded everyone of the long wandering in the desert after leaving Egypt.

People forgot how to plant wheat for bread and squeeze olives to make golden olive oil, but the old stories of Earth and animals were still told. And there were new stories as people learned the strange ways of their homes in the scattered lands of the world. At last, in the mid-1900s Jews were able to return to Palestine and recreate their old-new Israel. And that made for more storytelling, both new and old.

Many Jews loved their lost land so much that if they couldn't live in the Land of Israel, they wanted, at least, to be buried with a packet of soil from the Holy Land under their heads. This ancient Jewish cemetery in Prague, Czech Republic, holds crowded graves and many packets of soil from Israel. Years ago, the Jewish quarter in Prague was closed off by a wall. The buildings were so tall and tightly packed together that the cemetery was the only place the Jews could go to look up and see the sky. (Photo by Chaya M. Burstein)

Jonah: A Story from the Bible

God called on Jonah to go to Nineveh: "Warn the people of Nineveh that they will all die unless they change their ways and obey My laws," said God. "No, I won't," said Jonah. "I don't care what happens to Nineveh." Then Jonah hurried to the port and boarded a ship to get away from God's orders. But God caused a violent storm, and Jonah was thrown into the sea and swallowed by a giant fish, which may have been a whale. In the darkness inside the fish's belly Jonah got bounced around and scared out of his mind. "Okay, God," he cried, "Get me out of here! I give up. I'll go to Nineveh." The fish threw him up on dry land, and Jonah went to carry out God's command. Of course the people of

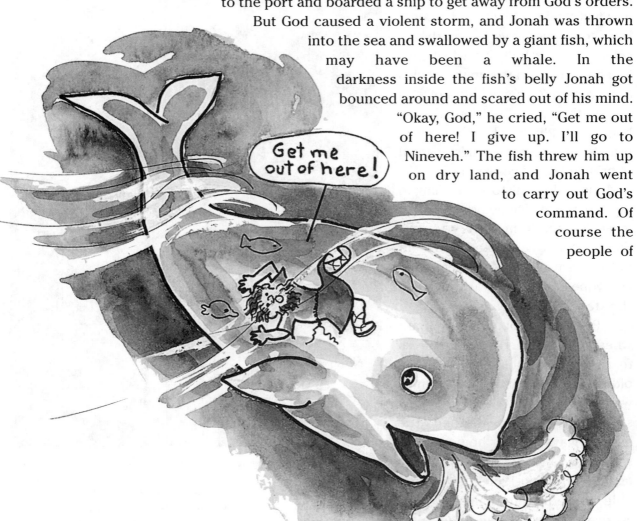

Nineveh all said they were sorry and promised to behave better. That made Jonah, who didn't care about Nineveh, very angry. He went out of the city and lay down to take a nap in the hot sun. A plant quickly grew up beside him and shaded him. It felt very good. But God sent a worm to attack the plant, and by the next morning the plant was dead. Jonah wept for the plant. Then God scolded him. "If you cry for a plant that grew up and died in one day, you should understand that I must have mercy on a great city full of people and many animals." God taught Jonah that he must care about people and animals, who deserve as much mercy and concern as a plant.

Mercy on Living Things: A Story from the Talmud

Judah the Prince was a learned, much-respected rabbi. One day, a calf that was being led to the butcher ran away and hid his head in the rabbi's lap. "Go back to the butcher," said Judah. "You were created to be slaughtered." At those words, a cry went up in heaven: "Because Rabbi Judah had no mercy on this living creature, he will be punished with much suffering." And so Rabbi Judah developed a terrible toothache. For 11 years he suffered with the toothache, until one day he saw his servant at work. She was sweeping a litter of kittens out of the house. "Stop!" cried Rabbi Judah. "Leave them alone. God has mercy on all living things." Because the rabbi finally showed mercy toward his fellow creatures, God had mercy on him, and his suffering ended.

The Boy Who Became the Baal Shem Tov

Little Israel Ben Eliezer felt choked in his schoolroom. All the other boys swayed back and forth over their books of Torah and Talmud and chanted loudly, but Israel felt the heavy prayers pressing against his head. They didn't make him feel closer to God or to God's wonderful world. He felt like he was in prison.

One day Israel quietly slipped off the bench and tiptoed out into the yard. He heard the birds singing, the sun warmed him, and suddenly he could breathe. He scrambled over the fence and ran up the dirt road that led from his village into the surrounding forest. Thorny bushes at the edge of the woods snatched at his legs. But he raced on quickly till he was in the shade of the tall trees. Thin shafts of sunlight poked through the leaves, but the dark shadows of tree trunks and bushes closed in around him. Spider webs and branches swept his hair as he ran. Except for the thud of his feet, it was quiet. The shouts of the peddlers in the market-place, the yelling of little children, the creaking of wagons—all gone. This was a strange, different world.

Finally, out of breath, he dropped onto a

moss-covered log and opened his eyes wide against the dimness. He sat as quietly as the forest around him. And as he sat, the forest creatures began to creep out. Two squirrels moved in the shadows and then bustled past him with fat, acorn-filled cheeks. A crow shrieked from a branch above and dropped twigs onto his head. Ferns uncurled around him, reaching up to the light. And then Israel began to hear voices. The tiny bell-like voice of a butterfly fluttering past; the deep drawl of a turtle in the grass; a raspy, scolding grasshopper beside him on the log— all of God's world was speaking to him! Even the rocks and caves beneath him rumbled their welcome.

Happiness filled Israel. This isn't a strange, different world, he thought. . . . It's God's world. All of it— the stuffy classroom and the marketplace, the forest and its creatures, and me. . . . We're all partners in God's wonderful world! He jumped up and spun around in a joyous, whirling dance. The squirrels, the crows, and the other forest creatures watched with shining eyes.

Little Israel got whacked with the teacher's ruler when he got back to school. But he didn't care. He grew up to become the Baal Shem Tov, the founder of Hasidism—a great religious leader who taught that joy in the earth and in nature and love of God and all of God's creatures are as important as study and scholarship. Instead of quietly swaying over his books, Israel began to sing and dance as he studied and prayed. To this day his followers also sing and dance to express their religious feelings.

A Fair Exchange: A Hasidic Folktale about True Justice

Hananiah the peddler worked his horse unmercifully. Through summer heat and freezing snowstorms, the horse dragged Hananiah and his heavy wagon from town to town. His only pay was a skimpy bag of oats and a pail of muddy water. Finally, the horse died and went straight to heaven. But instead of enjoying the green pastures, it stood at the gate and waited. Some time later Hananiah also died and also went up to heaven. "Aha!" cried the horse, barring Hananiah's way. "Now I'll make you pay for your cruelty!" The horse dragged Hananiah before the heavenly court and told the story of how his master had driven him, beaten him, and fed him only the poorest foods. "Tch, tch, tch," said the angels of the heavenly court. "The horse is right."

"No, no! Listen to me," Hananiah protested. "I worked just as hard as the horse, summer and winter. I was poor, too. I ate only black bread and herring, and I beat the lazy horse only to make him go."

"Tch, tch, tch," clucked the heavenly court. "The horse is right, but the peddler is right, too."

Just then a deep voice rumbled down from the highest part of heaven. "The peddler is right and the horse is right," said the voice. "Therefore both the peddler and the horse will return to Earth. But the horse will become the peddler and the peddler will become the horse."

The Land Is Not Ours to Lay Waste: A Story from the Midrash

On his way to do battle, the Roman emperor Hadrian was leading his army through the Land of Israel. He passed an old Jew planting fig-tree seedlings. "Why are you planting?" he asked. "You'll never live long enough to eat the fruit."

The old man answered, "Maybe I will and maybe I won't. But surely my children will eat the figs." After three years of war Hadrian came back on the same road and found the same farmer at work. The old man recognized Hadrian. He filled a basket with his first harvest of ripe figs and gave it to the emperor. Full of admiration, Hadrian filled the basket with gold coins and gave it back to the farmer.

Moral: The earth and its living creatures are ours to use and to care for. The earth will serve us and our children, and we must, in turn, preserve the earth.

Enough Is Enough: A Jewish Folktale about Caring for Living Things

An old woman trudged along the road carrying a heavy sack of potatoes over her shoulder. Soon a wagon drawn by a skinny horse rattled past her and stopped. "Climb on, Auntie," called the driver. She hoisted herself up and settled in beside him with a relieved sigh. They rolled along for a few minutes, then the driver glanced at his passenger. Surprised, he said, "Auntie, why are you still carrying the sack on your shoulder? Why don't you put it down?" "Oh, I can't," she said. "Your horse is so thin and he has you and me and this heavy wagon to pull. I can't make him pull my potatoes also!"

The Passover Bargain

excerpted and adapted from
Rifka Grows Up

BY CHAYA M. BURSTEIN

Such excitement in the home of Rifka and her younger brother Elli in the small Russian-Jewish town of Savran! Their favorite milk goat had given birth to two kids—a black-and-white-spotted male and a pure-white female. Elli, who was nine, fell in love with the tiny male and called him Samson, a hero's name. But young male goats in Savran didn't live long. They soon became the family's dinner. At the family's Passover seder, Elli found a way to save his little Samson. He stole the afikoman from the table and then used it to bargain for Samson's life. Here's what happened:

When the seder meal was cleared from the table, Papa leaned forward and lifted the cloth from the matzah dish. The *afikoman* was gone! Frowning ferociously, he pushed his glasses up on his forehead and looked around the table. When he reached red-faced Elli, the boy burst out laughing and said, "It was me. I stole it, and you never even noticed."

"Congratulations. You're an expert," said Papa. "But now I must have the *afikoman* back so that we can finish the seder."

Elli shook his head so hard that his earlocks bounced against his flushed cheeks.

"Name your price," Papa pleaded, "otherwise we'll have to sit all night."

The boy took a quick breath, looked across at his sister Rifka for help, and then exclaimed, "I want the little boy goat!"

Nobody spoke for a moment. Then all the grownups seemed to burst out scolding and arguing at the same time.

"That's silly. . . . What's the matter with you?" Aunt Miriam shrilled, "Can't you ask for a new shirt or a penknife or some chocolate like a normal boy?"

"Elli, that's not a fair request," Papa protested. "The kid has no purpose except to be butchered. He'll never give milk, and he'll eat us out of house and home. Now be a good boy and ask for something else."

"He'll climb up and chew on our thatched roof again. Don't be a child," Mama scolded.

Uncle Ephraim added to the general background noise, blinking with astonishment and murmuring, "Well, well. Well!"

Elli got redder and redder. His lower lip stuck out stubbornly, his eyes were watery, and he just kept shaking his head from side to side.

"Me too, I like the little goat," Berelleh piped up, then hushed as Aunt Miriam raised her broad hand.

"It's a holiday of freedom," Rifka said thoughtfully. "Elli is only asking that Samson should be free to live."

"Aha—another attorney for the defense," Mama groaned.

"A dumb animal does not understand freedom," Papa stated.

"Oh, Papa, you should watch him gallop down the street pushing a barrel, or playing tag with Elli in the meadow beside the clay pit. He's so happy, he's almost laughing out loud. And then he looks so sad when we close the shed door at night. He must know about freedom."

"That's enough talk. We must finish this seder," Papa said firmly. "Elli, this is my final offer. We'll keep the male goat until

DEFINITION, PLEASE!

The *afikoman* is one of the three symbolic pieces of matzah placed in the center of the Passover seder table.

the fall, until the holiday of Sukkot is over. Maybe by then something will have happened to the town billy goat—who can tell?"

Elli sagged. This was Papa's "I've had enough" voice. He pulled the *afikoman* from under his jacket and handed it across the table.

The wine cups were filled. The adults began to sing again, and after a while Elli and Rifka joined in. When the candles were burned down to stubs, the family reached the final, best-loved seder song—*Had Gadya*—"One Only Kid."

Elli smiled across at Rifka as they sang in a wailing singsong about a small goat, bought by Father for two zuzim, which was eaten by a cat, which was bitten by a dog, which was beaten by a stick . . . and on and on . . . until final justice was handed down by the Holy One.

In the shed, the small male kid flicked a fly from his ear and snuggled more tightly against his mother and sister.

At Dawn

BY RACHEL BLUESTEIN

translated from the Hebrew
BY CHAYA M. BURSTEIN

In the late 1800s, more and more Jews began to return to the Land of Israel. They swung pickaxes to build roads and pushed plows through the rock-filled fields. Rachel Bluestein came to Palestine from Russia in the 1920s to help build a Jewish home-land and to write poems that told about her love of the land.

A jug of water in my hand,
   On my shoulder
A basket, hoe, and rake.
To the far fields, to work, I go.
On my right the guarding mountains,
Ahead the wide fields spread,
And in my heart my twenty springtimes sing.
May this be mine until the end,
Your grain fields gleaming in the sun
And the dust of your roads. My land.

We sometimes forget that everything we wear and use and eat grows in a long, complicated chain from the earth. One Shabbat eve, a boy called Aaron follows the links all the way back to the original Oneness.

Challah

BY SHARON DUNN AND
JOHN J. CLAYTON

Every Friday at sundown, Dad, Mom, and I gather to say the blessings for the Sabbath—we call it *Shabbat*, that's Hebrew—or *Shabbos*, that's Yiddish.

The house smells sweet—it's the scent of bread just baked and still warm. We light the *Shabbos* candles and raise the cup of wine. Next we will bless our challah, the braided bread I love.

But this *Shabbos* is different.

My dad (who is always teaching me) asks, "See our challah, Aaron! Two beautiful loaves. Just how many people do you think it took to bring this challah to our table?"

"Simple," I say. "Two. Mom made them this afternoon, and I helped!"

"Yes, you and Mom made challah—but who else helped?"

The ingredients! "Well," I say, "there's everyone who made the flour, the oil, the sugar, and the yeast. And the farmer who raised the chickens to lay the eggs. Oh, and someone grew the sesame seeds we sprinkle on top!"

"Who else?" Dad is smiling at Mom. This is his idea of fun, this kind of question!

"Well," I say, "the supermarket guys."

"And the supermarket—how did they get all the stuff? And before that? How does the wheat get to the flour maker, the miller?"

DEFINITION, PLEASE!

Yiddish is a language that has been spoken by Jews in much of Europe for centuries, and is still spoken by some ultra-Orthodox Jews today. It's a mixture of old German, Hebrew, and bits of Russian, Polish, and English. To add to the mish-mash—it's written in the Hebrew alphabet.

"Trucks, trains?"

"Aha!" my father exclaims. "Now we're getting somewhere. And who made the trucks and the trains?" He goes on. "What about the people who made the wheels and the tires?"

I can do this! This is fun. So I say, "Okay! Okay, Dad. And don't forget the farmer who plowed the wheat fields with a tractor—and the guys who made the tractors! And," I add, "the school bus that takes kids to school so that their parents can work!"

"That's a stretch," Dad says. "But okay! How about the teachers who teach kids math so that they can become engineers to design better equipment for the foundry or for the milling or for the trucking?"

Dad and I keep going, and Mom joins in, too:

"Seed. Did you know it's taken thousands of years to develop the kinds of seeds we make flour from?"

"Fertilizer—lots!"

"Our oven—think of all the people it took to make that!"

"Electricity we baked with—and what about the fuel to make the electricity? And the linemen to keep the wires working?"

"Paper bags to hold our flour and sugar—all those trees had to be cut, and then the paper had to be made, and then the bags from the paper."

"Bauxite mined for our aluminum baking sheets."

"The bowl in which the dough rose: the people who molded, glazed, and fired the clay. The digging of the clay itself."

"That's a million people already!" laughs my mom. "More! Oh, and wait a minute," she says. "What about the recipe? I didn't invent the recipe. I got it from Amy, and Amy got it from Debbie, and Debbie got it from her mother-in-law, Larry's mother. Challah recipes go back and back and back. And the braids. Challah is braided. I wonder where the braids come from?"

"And the blessing you say, Hannah, when you put it in the oven—that makes it challah, 'bread of praise,' and not just egg bread!" My dad's voice rises. "We're eating the bread of our Eastern European Jewish ancestors and saying the blessings of our Israelite ancestors. Think of all the people! And the blessing that makes baking the bread a mitzvah—following God's commandment—is from the Torah. So it's the wisdom of a community that goes back thousands of years—at least to Moses."

Mom gets a big card from a kitchen drawer and hands it to me. "Here's the recipe itself."

"Ah," Dad sighs. "It's written in English, a language that comes from many other people, from tribes who pushed the Celts out of England. But their language has been blended with French that came in when the Normans conquered England and Latin that came in just before Shakespeare was born." Sometimes my Dad can't stop. . . . "Now! Now we arrive at the truly miraculous," he says.

"To make that loaf of challah, you need not just people, right? You need the land itself. You need the laws of gravity. And what about the laws of growth! Not to mention the dance of particles, the different wave lengths of everything by which the world comes to us: visible light so we can see the bread; heat so we can bake the bread. Air itself for dough to rise in . . . and the smell. Ah, the smell." His voice goes quiet. "Then why not thank all these things and people instead of God?" he asks me.

"Why?" I say because I truly do not know.

"Because," he says, "it's all forms of a single energy that makes the challah and makes us. It's as if all this streams forth out of an original Oneness. We are given all this—and we are part of the gift."

We say, in Hebrew, the blessing over the bread as our hands touch the loaves. "Blessed are You, Lord our God, Ruler of the universe, who brings forth bread from the earth."

Baruch attah Adonai, Eloheinu melekh ha-olam, ha-motzi lechem min ha-aretz.

The challah tastes more wonderful than ever tonight.

It melts on my tongue and I think of every bit of it as it fills me.

My father puts his hand on my head to bless me, too. We will sing to angels to bring us peace for this *Shabbat*. That is how we begin our day of heaven on Earth every week. Because that's what *Shabbat* is supposed to be—as if one day a week we can live in heaven. Mom and Dad hold hands. Joyously we sing *Shalom Aleikhem*—"Peace to You."

Now we will eat our supper.

The candles stay on the table, not to be moved. They will burn down and out, hours from now when I am asleep.

And there will be *Shabbos* next week, and next, and on and on. . . .

Stories with Roots of a Different Kind

Some of the Bible's teachings vary and may seem confusing. It is written that we may use the earth, but we must also care for it. We also read that we must fill the earth with people and rule over other living things. And a third message warns us that the earth belongs to God, and God permits us humans to share it and use it, but only for a while.

Many Native Americans believed in a Great Spirit who cared about the whole world. But they also saw gods in nature, in the waters, the skies, and the sun and the moon. They trapped and killed animals for food, but they thanked the spirits of the animals for feeding them. The great trees of the forest were like respected older brothers, and the plunging waterfalls were a source of life. Though we don't accept the idea of the existence of many gods, some of the Native

American stories, with their love and respect for nature, may help us to understand our place among the living creatures of the world. They are stories with roots of a different kind.

The writer Jaime de Angulo describes a group of animals that are bedding down after a long walk. They call out "good night" to all the world around them:

Then Bear called, "Good night, Mountains, you must protect us tonight. We are strangers but we are good people. We don't mean harm to anybody. Good night, Mister Pine Tree. We are camping under you. You must protect us tonight. Good night, Mister Owl. I guess this is your home where we are camped. We are good people, we are not looking for trouble, we are just traveling. Good night, Chief Rattlesnake. Good night, everyone. Good night, Grass People, we have spread our bed right on top of you. Good night, Ground, we are lying right on your face. You must take care of us, we want to live a long time."

—from the book *Indian Tales*
by Jaime de Angulo

Snoqualmie Falls in western Washington state is named for the Indian tribe that once had winter villages along the Snoqualmie River. These Indians had no form of agriculture and no domesticated animals except the dog. They lived by hunting, fishing, and gathering plants and berries. The tribe built wooden houses, often big enough for several families. Today this scenic area is popular with hikers. (Photo by Chaya M. Burstein)

The Snoqualmie Indians of the American Northwest see holiness in a great waterfall, whose water tumbles from snow-covered mountains down into a deep pool. A gray mist rises from the clash of waters, filling the gorge below and covering the rocks and surrounding forests. "The first man and woman were created here, from out of this water," say the Snoqualmie.

The Osage Indians, who once lived in the American Midwest, sent their young boys out alone into the forest. They were to gain wisdom from the trees and animals. They might have dreams and visions that would help them know which paths to take to get out of the forest and which paths to take in their future lives.

We have much to learn from Native Americans about living in partnership with the earth. Chief Seattle, the Indian after whom the city of Seattle was named, was an eloquent teacher. He was a leader of two tribes—his mother's, called the Duwamish, and his father's, called the Suquamish. When he was asked to sell the tribes' lands to the U.S. government in 1855, he answered with some painful, difficult questions and warnings. He said: "How can you buy or sell the sky, the land? If we do not own the air and the sparkle of the water, how can you buy them? Every part of this earth is sacred to my people. Every shining pine needle. Every mist in the dark woods. Every humming insect. Will you teach your children what we have taught our children, that the earth is our mother? The earth does not belong to humans. Humans belong to the earth. If we sell you our land, love it as we have loved it. Care for it as we have cared for it."

What would Chief Seattle, who died in 1866, and his daughter, nicknamed Princess Angeline by European-Americans, think seeing the Indians' old hunting grounds today?

TAKE A HIKE IN THE PARK OR WOODS

ECO-ACTIVITY
ECO-ACTIVITY

Take a tree or bird book along if you like to identify what you see. Sit quietly on a rock or a log for a while like Israel Ben Eliezer—the Baal Shem Tov—and watch the sun sparkle through the leaves of the trees. If you're very quiet a squirrel or chipmunk may hurry past or a turtle may trudge along. And birds will dart back and forth through the trees. Sniff the leafy, mossy smells of our good Earth. And if it's your first hike of the season, say a prayer of thanks for the wonderfulness of the natural world. But . . . hey, take your sandwich wrappings and other garbage home with you.

If you find the right tree, hiking can be very relaxing. Just ask Naomi. (Photo by Chaya M. Burstein)

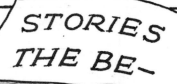

NICE STORIES. I GUESS YOU DO CARE ABOUT ME AND MY CREATURES A LITTLE BIT.

MORE THAN A LITTLE BIT. I LOVE WALKING IN THE WOODS AND DIGGING IN THE GARDEN.

AND I LIKE FEEDING THE BIRDS AND PLAYING CATCH WITH SPOT. LIKE THE BIBLE TELLS US, WE'RE USING YOU BUT WE'RE ALSO TAKING CARE OF YOU.

NOT EXACTLY! YOU HUMANS AREN'T JUST USING ME - YOU'RE USING ME UP! FOR EXAMPLE - DO YOU KNOW WHAT YOUR GLOBAL WARMING IS DOING TO MY BEAUTIFUL GLACIERS? THEY'RE STARTING TO MELT!

WHAT? ARE WE RESPONSIBLE FOR GLACIER'S TOO? I NEVER EVEN SAW A GLACIER. IT'S NOT MY FAULT IF THEY'RE MELTING.

TCH, TCH, TCH... HOW COME IT'S NEVER YOUR FAULT?

6

The Earth's Turn

PHEW! FINALLY IT'S MY TURN. WELL, AHEM, HERE GOES!

I've been around for a long time and I've seen lots of planets, so I gotta admit—I'm the best in the solar system! I've got atmosphere with oxygen to breathe. I've got perfect temperatures for all living things, from Eskimos and polar bears in the North to penguins in Antarctica to Pygmies at the equator. I've got tropical jungles and cool pine forests, giant redwoods and dwarf fir trees. Lakes, rivers, oceans. Millions of kinds of animals, birds, fish, and insects enjoy my facilities. Without boasting, I can tell you that I'm a Garden of Eden, just like the Bible says. I'm a colorful jewel of a planet peacefully spinning around the sun. I'm perfect!

Anyhow, I used to be perfect.

About 100,000 years ago, you human beings started to spread across my surface like an itchy case of chicken pox. It wasn't a problem. Hey, I have nothing against people! There's room on Earth for all kinds of living things. Humans picked berries, nuts, and grains to eat. They fished and hunted and ate animals. And after a while they started to make tools for chopping, scraping, and cutting. Tens of thousands of years later they planted seeds to grow barley and wheat and even saved seeds and grain for the winter. Smart, those humans. Next, they were using animals to pull their plows and wagons, and had animals provide them with milk, meat, fur, and wool. They dumped their garbage—old fish bones, torn furs, and other waste—outside their homes, where insects and bacteria digested the garbage and turned it into rich soil. Sometimes the rotting garbage made them sick, so they picked up and moved to a new site.

Now and then humans did stupid things. They would sharpen sticks for spears and make heavy stone axes and go off to attack other humans. They would burn huts, steal from each other, and kill each other. That didn't make sense, but it didn't bother me. I'm the earth. I kept my balance.

Too Smart, Too Bad

About 250 years ago, humans started getting too smart. They had an industrial revolution—which means they started building machines to work for them. They chopped down trees and burned wood to make power to run their machines. Then they started to dig tunnels under my skin and bring up coal to burn, to make even more power for the machines. More and more people were born, and more trees and coal were needed to feed the machines. Smoke from all the fuel pushed up into my atmosphere, and trash and junk and waste from all the new products piled up on my soil and in my water. But a lot of it couldn't be digested by my natural cleanup crews. Some of the metals and chemicals the humans used wouldn't decay at all. They just kept piling up around the cities, spilling into rivers, and soaking through my skin.

People started pumping oil from deep inside me. They built trains and cars, got rid of their horses, camels, and donkeys, and started zipping around belching exhaust fumes. Phew! Now it smells terrible. Besides, you know what that exhaust is doing to my air? Ruining it!

And terrible things started happening to my other living things while you humans were having your industrial revolution. Animals started getting butchered or squeezed off their land. Once hundreds of thousands of buffalo roamed the Great Plains of North America, and millions of carrier pigeons filled the sky. Then people came along with guns and started slaughtering them. There are still a few protected herds of buffalo, but the carrier pigeons are gone—extinct. In Africa, the mountain forests where gorillas live are being cut down to provide lumber and to clear land for farming. The gorillas are dying. Soon you'll only find them in the zoo. Elephants are

DID YOU KNOW?

I'm the Blue Planet. Three quarters of me is covered in water, most of it ocean. But just because there's so much ocean doesn't mean it's okay to dump stuff there. People's trash, industrial metals and chemicals, used engine oil from cars and trucks—they all hurt my marine plants and animals. My great big oceans are becoming a mess.

being crowded into smaller and smaller areas as humans take over the land. And hundreds of other species of birds, animals, insects, and plants have become extinct in the last hundred years.

And this business of human wars. It used to be rocks, boiling oil, and bows and arrows. I could live with that. But today it's huge steel tanks, aircraft carriers, napalm, intercontinental ballistic missiles. You're even splitting my atoms to make weapons. You guys are getting better and better at killing each other, and I'm the one who has to suffer. Wars kill people, animals, trees, and me—the earth!

I'm not selfish. I'm willing to share my good stuff, my air and trees and fertile soil. But you guys are going too far. You're taking much more from me than you're giving back. If you keep doing that you'll ruin me and yourselves!

Hey, I'm not the only one who yells at you humans for being so know-it-all and wasteful. In the Bible, in the Book of Job, God scolds human beings because they think they can understand and judge whatever happens in the world:

> *Where were you when I laid the*
>   *foundations of the earth?*
> *Speak, if you have understanding . . .*
> *Do you know who laid the earth's cornerstone?*
> *When the morning stars sang together*
> *And all the children of God shouted for joy . . . ?*
> *How is the light parted, or*
> *The east wind scattered over the earth?*
> *Is it by your wisdom that the hawk*
>   *grows pinions*
> *And spreads his wings to the south?*
> *Does the eagle soar at your command,*
> *Building his nest high, dwelling on the rock,*
> *On the peak of a rock fortress?*

(Job 38:4, 6–7, 24 and 39:26–28)

And in the 12th century, the smart Jewish philosopher called Maimonides wrote that a person should know his or her place and not mistakenly believe that the whole universe exists only for human beings.

About 800 years later, in the 20th century, the scientist Rachel Carson suggested that we're behaving as though the whole universe truly exists only for humankind. She asked, "Can we have a clean environment if we have an ever-increasing standard of living?"

So please, you guys, think it over—for your sakes and mine. You need to ask yourselves: Is more, faster, bigger stuff always better?

Time to Think It Over

DEFINITION, PLEASE!

Job is the hero of the Book of Job. He is a very righteous man who suffers a whole lot—for no reason that he or anybody else can figure out. For thousands of years, sages and scholars have been wondering about the meaning of this Bible story. I'm only the earth, you know, so don't ask *me!*

ECO-ACTIVITY

ECO-ACTIVITY

TEE SHIRTS TALK

Help the earth! Spread the word with a tee-shirt slogan. Slogans don't usually explain anything, but they catch people's attention. (*Then* you can explain.) Using a stencil is one way to make a tee shirt talk. You can also draw your slogan and design directly on the tee shirt, instead of using the stiff paper.

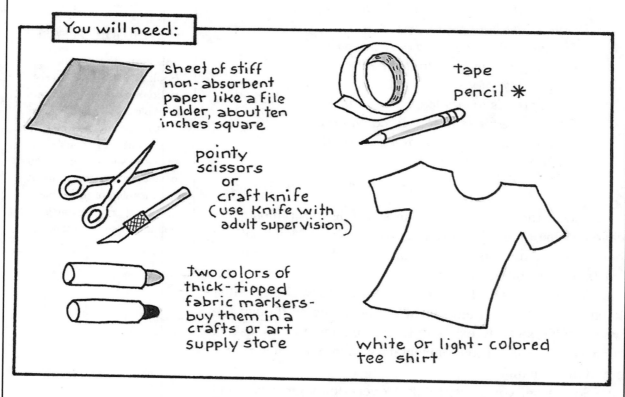

You will need:

sheet of stiff non-absorbent paper like a file folder, about ten inches square

tape
pencil ✱

pointy scissors or craft knife (use knife with adult supervision)

two colors of thick-tipped fabric markers- buy them in a crafts or art supply store

white or light-colored tee shirt

✱ to make the drawing easier you can buy a stencil for drawing the letters at an art supply store

ECO-ACTIVITY

1

Draw the slogan or design on the stiff paper. The design should be no bigger than ten inches square. The lines of the letters should be at least ¼ inch wide.

10 inches

¼ inch

10 inches

2

Use the scissors or craft knife to cut out the design you've drawn on the stiff paper.

Some design suggestions

DON'T DUMP
COMPOST!

RECYCLE
SAVE TREES

HELP OUR HOME
RECYCLE

3

Tape the stiff paper to the tee-shirt. With the fabric markers paint the design onto the tee shirt through the cut out spaces.

4

Remove the paper. Let the paint dry, and then wear the shirt proudly.

THE EARTH IS SICK

COME ON MR/MS EARTH, AREN'T YOU BEING KINDA SELFISH? THIS INDUSTRIAL REVOLUTION WAS A GOOD THING. WE DON'T GO TO THE WELL FOR WATER OR WASH OUR CLOTHES IN THE RIVER. WE CAN PLAY COMPUTER GAMES AND TAKE A PLANE TO SEE OUR GRANDPARENTS AT HOLIDAY TIME. IT'S GREAT!

KIDDO, HOW LONG HAVE YOU BEEN AROUND? TEN YEARS? TWELVE YEARS? I'VE BEEN AROUND FOR 6,000 YEARS, OR BILLIONS OF YEARS. EITHER WAY I CAN TAKE A MUCH LONGER VIEW OF WHAT'S HAPPENING.

FOR MOST OF MY LIFE THINGS KEPT GETTING BETTER. I MATURED FROM A CLOUD OF HOT GAS INTO THE GREEN, PLEASANT EARTH YOU KNOW TODAY. BUT IN THE LAST FEW CENTURIES I'VE CHANGED. I'M FALLING APART.

NO, YOU'RE NOT. YOU'RE GREAT JUST THE WAY YOU ARE.

BUT I WON'T STAY THE WAY I AM. I'M SICK. AND IF WE DON'T WORK TO MAKE ME BETTER I'LL GET SICKER. AND THAT WILL MAKE THINGS BAD FOR ALL LIVING THINGS— INCLUDING YOU.

7 What's Happening to the Earth?

The First People

They began to develop in Africa 2–3 million years ago and later spread to Asia and Europe about 500,000 years ago.

In chapter 2, the beginning of the earth was described as the Bible does in the story of Creation. Today, some geologists and archaeologists suggest that each of the Bible's six days of Creation may have lasted millions of years instead of 24 hours—and on the sixth "day" human beings evolved. In three bird's-eye views, let's see what changes we've made in our environment since the first human beings began to live on Earth. Check the report cards to compare how we've been doing.

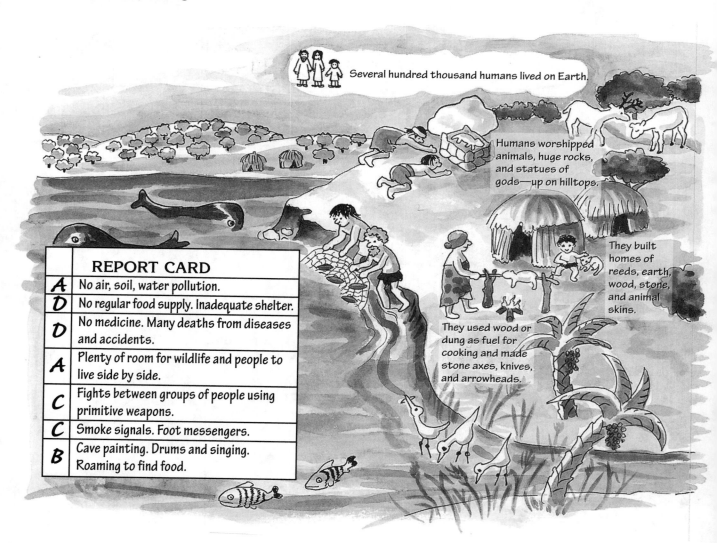

Several hundred thousand humans lived on Earth.

Humans worshipped animals, huge rocks, and statues of gods—up on hilltops.

They built homes of reeds, earth, wood, stone, and animal skins.

They used wood or dung as fuel for cooking and made stone axes, knives, and arrowheads.

	REPORT CARD
A	No air, soil, water pollution.
D	No regular food supply. Inadequate shelter.
D	No medicine. Many deaths from diseases and accidents.
A	Plenty of room for wildlife and people to live side by side.
C	Fights between groups of people using primitive weapons.
C	Smoke signals. Foot messengers.
B	Cave painting. Drums and singing. Roaming to find food.

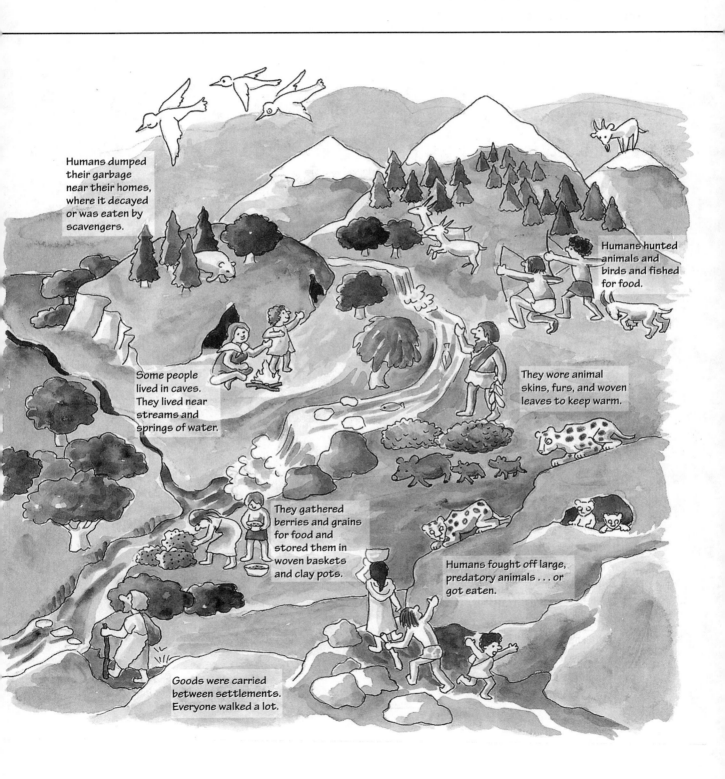

Humans dumped their garbage near their homes, where it decayed or was eaten by scavengers.

Humans hunted animals and birds and fished for food.

Some people lived in caves. They lived near streams and springs of water.

They wore animal skins, furs, and woven leaves to keep warm.

They gathered berries and grains for food and stored them in woven baskets and clay pots.

Humans fought off large, predatory animals . . . or got eaten.

Goods were carried between settlements. Everyone walked a lot.

People 250 Years Ago

They lived before motor-driven machines were invented and big factories were developed.

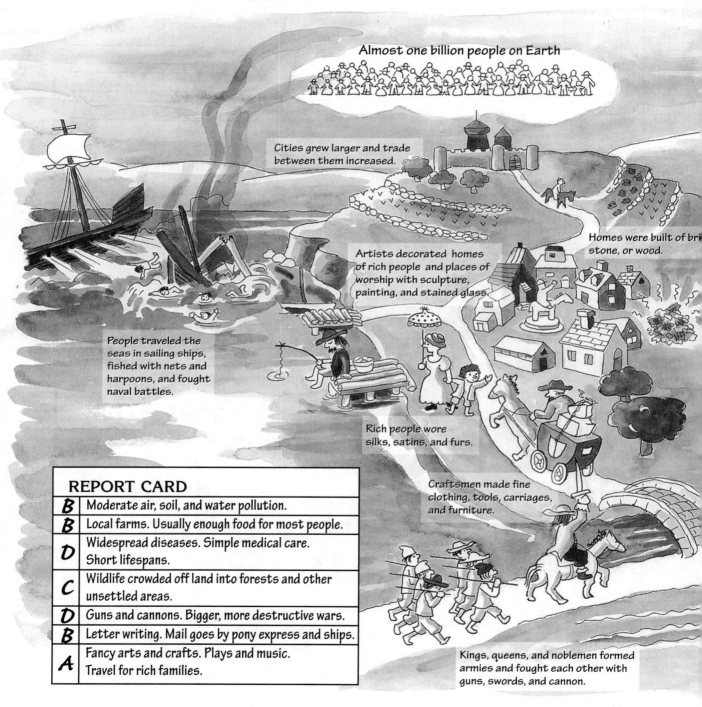

Almost one billion people on Earth

Cities grew larger and trade between them increased.

Homes were built of bri stone, or wood.

Artists decorated homes of rich people and places of worship with sculpture, painting, and stained glass.

People traveled the seas in sailing ships, fished with nets and harpoons, and fought naval battles.

Rich people wore silks, satins, and furs.

Craftsmen made fine clothing, tools, carriages, and furniture.

Kings, queens, and noblemen formed armies and fought each other with guns, swords, and cannon.

REPORT CARD	
B	Moderate air, soil, and water pollution.
B	Local farms. Usually enough food for most people.
D	Widespread diseases. Simple medical care. Short lifespans.
C	Wildlife crowded off land into forests and other unsettled areas.
D	Guns and cannons. Bigger, more destructive wars.
B	Letter writing. Mail goes by pony express and ships.
A	Fancy arts and crafts. Plays and music. Travel for rich families.

Garbage was dumped in the streets and rivers, or piled up outside of town.

Many big trees were cut down for lumber and firewood.

Wild animals lived in the forests, and people hunted them for food and fun.

People raised chickens, geese, sheep, goats, cows, and pigs for food and clothing.

Wells and cisterns were dug to hold water for farms and homes.

Waterwheels and windmills ground grain.

Farmers grew fruits, vegetables, and grains. They used oxen, donkeys, and horses to pull plows.

People used ferries or built bridges of wood, metal, or stone and made roads of earth, wood, or stone.

Wagons hauled goods and passengers. And people walked a lot, carrying packs.

People Today

They inhabit a world where it's possible to travel fast and far and to communicate quickly with many people.

Six-and-a-quarter billion people on Earth

"Factory" fishing ships with huge nets empty much of the sea of large fish.

Smoke from burning fuels and chemicals pollutes the air and damages the ozone layer.

Half the world's people live in cities.

Oil tankers crisscross the oceans providing cheap, plentiful fuel. "Oil spills" harm marine life.

Fields and orchards are sprayed with pesticides. They protect the fruit but often harm other living things.

	REPORT CARD
F	Heavy air, soil, and water pollution.
B	Large farms. More food shipped long distances to more people.
B	Good medical care in advanced countries. Longer lifespans possible.
F	Wildlife losses as open space disappears.
F	Modern warfare killing more people and harming the environment.
A	Phones and computers.
A	Popular entertainment and speedy travel available in modern countries.

Changes

You've just seen three illustrations full of information—too much information to remember. But one thing is clear. Great changes have happened in human life and in the earth's environment over the past 100,000 years. Can these changes seriously affect our huge, solid, comfortable spinning Earth? To judge, let's take the biggest factors, one by one, and find out more about them. We'll look at human population, water, earth, and air.

HUMAN POPULATION

We believe that several hundred thousand people lived on the earth 100,000 years ago. About 99,750 years later (250 years ago) our numbers had slowly grown to almost one billion. And today, human population numbers have jumped to more than six billion! So it took millions of years for our population to reach almost one billion, but then in the next 250 years we added more than five billion people. On a chart, the increase looks like this:

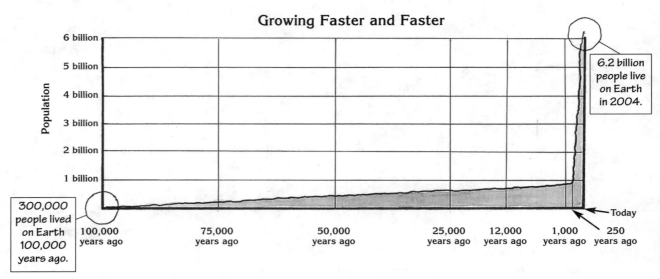

Note: The chart is a little out of scale to show the changes clearly.

Why have our numbers grown so quickly, especially in the last 100 years? The answer goes way back 10,000 years, when the first smart humans got a head start on the other animals. They learned to plant crops and, later, to domesticate animals so that people had a ready food supply. Fewer children or adults died of hunger, and the population grew. Cities grew, too, as more food was transported from the ever-bigger farms.

A giant leap happened with the industrial revolution, starting about 250 years ago. Scientific advances and mechanical inventions enabled people to produce many tons more of food, clothing, and other goods. Medical care began to improve as well. More babies stayed healthy and grew up, and they had more babies who stayed healthy and grew up, and they had. . . . Now there are more than six billion of us!

What is this growth doing to our sturdy, beloved Mr/Ms Earth? At first humans had no more effect on the earth

than lions, rabbits, owls, or other living things. But as our population grew, we began to spread over the earth's surface. We needed more food so farmers chopped down forests to clear farmland. We needed water for farming, for our livestock, and also for industry. Slowly we tapped more and more of the fresh water in lakes and rivers, and the water of underground reservoirs. Waste from farms, homes, and factories was dumped right back into the water. (See more about trash and pollution in chapter 9.)

As people spread into the forests and jungles, they began to crowd out other animals. Gorillas in Africa have been squeezed into a small corner of their former territory. When the home areas of elephants were taken over by people, the elephants sometimes rampaged through the villages, and people shot them. Whole species of animals, birds, insects, and plants died out as their natural environment was

destroyed. Of course humans have been killing off other species for thousands of years. Cavemen finished off the woolly mammoths, and white settlers on the American Great Plains killed almost all the buffaloes. But some scientists believe that more species have died off in this past century than at any time since the extinction of the dinosaurs 65 million years ago.

WATER

We're lucky to be living on this planet instead of Mars or Jupiter. More than two-thirds of the earth's surface is water. And we're also lucky because we have just as much fresh (non-salty) water today as we did when the first human beings roamed the forests. That sounds great. We haven't used it all up. But we're dividing it among many more thirsty people than ever, as well as the many factories and farms. Lakes and rivers in many parts of the world are shrinking. For example, the town of Muynak in Uzbekistan used to be a fishing town on the shore of the Aral Sea. But streams feeding the lake were diverted to provide water for farm fields, and the lake slowly dried out. Today Muynak sits in a desert, miles from the nearest water. A fishing boat still stands high and dry at the end of one of the streets.

In other parts of the world water is used wastefully. Each time you and I flush a toilet we're using as much water as a person in a less developed country has for one day—for *all* drinking, cooking, and washing. If we let the water run while we brush our teeth, use sprinklers to water our lawns, and wash clothes or dishes before the machine is full, we're wasting gallons and gallons of water.

Our precious supply of fresh water in streams, rivers, and lakes is being polluted by sewage and chemicals that flow into them from factories and by pesticides and fertilizers that run off farmers' fields. And if such waste is dumped directly onto the ground and gets mixed with rain, it filters into the earth to pollute underground reservoirs of fresh water.

Almost all the water on Earth is salty, ocean water. When you fly or sail over it, it seems to go on forever. But even our huge, endless oceans are in danger, especially at their shore lines. We're messing them up by dumping waste into them, just as we do into our lakes and rivers. The water is not only getting dirty—whole sections of ocean are being emptied of living things because sea plants and animals can't grow in the polluted water. Overfishing is emptying the seas, too. (More about this in the next chapter.)

EARTH

Do you like to lie on your stomach in the grass and smell the sweet, damp smell of the earth? Or flip over on your back and chew a stalk of grass as you look up through the leaves of the trees to the faraway sky? The earth under us feels good, smells good—and it's a totally reliable, solid part of our world. Or is it? Well, not exactly, because we're changing the earth just as we're changing the water and the air. One change is in the size of the earth's forests and jungles.

So remember, when I breathe in, you breathe out.

Once a major part of the earth was covered by trees. They are the lungs of the planet. Trees breathe in and absorb from the air a natural gas called carbon dioxide, which they use to make carbohydrates for their food. Then the trees give off or breathe out oxygen, which we and other living things need to breathe. Forests serve in another way—they're home to about two-thirds of the earth's plant and animal species. But as our human population grows, and we need more space and more wood, we

Giant sequoia trees ("redwoods") once covered the inland mountains of California and thrived in the drizzle and mist of the Oregon and Washington coasts. We still enjoy Sequoia National Park and several redwood forests, but most of the huge stretches of giant trees have been cut down. Strange but true—the giant sequoia grows from a seed as tiny as the head of a pin. (Photo by keeweechic. Courtesy of virtualtourist.com)

chop down trees. Each year we cut down hundreds of acres of forest—added together, that's as much land as the state of Florida.

Natural climate change has caused fertile land to become desert. But people cause deserts to grow, too. Fertile land is turning into desert as the roots of cut-down trees die. And without roots to hold it in place, the soil is blown away or washed away, leaving only rock.

In Central Africa the earth is damaged as too many people try to live on the same scarce patches of land. Shepherds trying to feed their families graze their cattle or goats over fragile grasslands. The animals eat the grass down to the roots, and both grass and soil are lost. Other once-fertile lands become less productive as they're poisoned by pesticides, large amounts of chemical fertilizer, and the trash and waste that are dumped on it.

AIR

Take a deep breath. If you're a city kid, chances are that you'll get a whiff of car exhaust or smoke. We burn fossil fuels—oil, natural gas, and coal—to run our machinery, cars, school buses, trucks, and planes, or to generate electricity. The exhaust from chimneys and tailpipes rises into the air. In some places the air is so thick with pollutants or smog that you'd better stay indoors on a windless day, especially if you have asthma or even a bad cold.

And there's another air problem. Pollutants in the air combine with moisture in the air and form acids that are washed down to the earth in the form of "acid rain." Acid rain is like watering your house plants with laundry bleach, and it has killed whole forests in Canada and the northeastern United States.

Scientists are concerned that some chemicals like freon gas from air conditioners and the chemicals in fumigants (pumped into the soil to kill insect pests) are thinning the ozone layer. This layer forms a blanket around the earth that protects us from the sun's harmful, ultraviolet radiation. A thinner ozone layer may cause more eye problems and skin cancer.

Unfortunately, there's more. There's the human interference with the "greenhouse effect." The greenhouse effect is a good, natural process by which the earth's atmosphere conserves its heat. Without this process we'd all freeze to death. But when too much heat is retained, our environment is negatively affected by "global warming." The illlustration on the next page shows what's happening.

If you live in Minnesota, a little warming may not seem like a bad idea. But a change of only a few degrees in temperature can cause less snow to fall and glaciers to shrink. Higher average temperatures can affect trees, animals, and insects. They can alter sea levels, shift the direction of the winds, and seriously change the climates of the world.

FOSSIL FUELS

Several hundred million years ago, during the time of the dinosaurs, giant trees and plants grew over much of the earth. As they died, they were buried under many thousands of feet of earth and water. The heat and pressure slowly cooked some of the organic material into petroleum (oil) and natural gas. Other material fossilized and became coal. Ancient vegetation and other organic material are the sources of the fuel that runs our machines today. But when these fuels are burned they give off most of the carbon dioxide produced on earth. And excessive amounts of carbon dioxide pollute our air and help cause global warming.

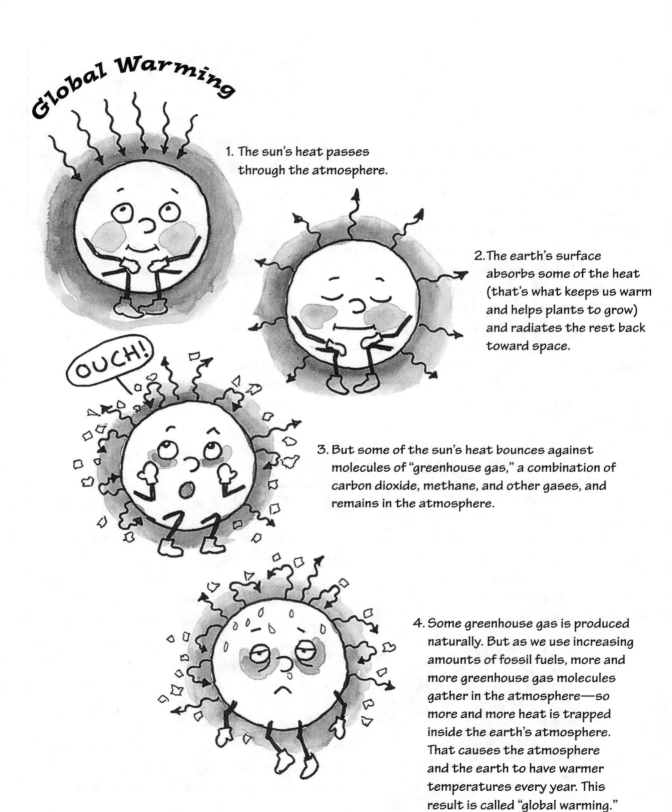

Global Warming

1. The sun's heat passes through the atmosphere.

2. The earth's surface absorbs some of the heat (that's what keeps us warm and helps plants to grow) and radiates the rest back toward space.

OUCH!

3. But some of the sun's heat bounces against molecules of "greenhouse gas," a combination of carbon dioxide, methane, and other gases, and remains in the atmosphere.

4. Some greenhouse gas is produced naturally. But as we use increasing amounts of fossil fuels, more and more greenhouse gas molecules gather in the atmosphere—so more and more heat is trapped inside the earth's atmosphere. That causes the atmosphere and the earth to have warmer temperatures every year. This result is called "global warming."

A PUSH FOR ECO-FRIENDLY MANUFACTURING

The European Union (a family of democratic, European countries) is demanding that manufacturers be responsible for recycling or reusing products that until now have been thrown away as trash. Stuff like old, unwanted refrigerators, TV sets, cars, and computers must be taken apart. Then their materials must be reused or disposed of in ways that don't harm the environment.

Ecology News Flashes

SOME GOOD THINGS ARE HAPPENING!

ORGANIC FARMERS DECLARE WAR

Some farmers in California and Washington, and many other parts of the United States and the world, are growing their crops only with fertilizer made of natural products like compost or manure. And they don't use chemical pesticides. Instead the farmers choose to use natural predators to kill harmful rodents and insects. They bring these natural predators to their fields to make war on the harmful insects, weeds, and diseases. We get less pollution and healthier food.

Germany, an ecology superstar

Germany leads the world in getting energy from windmills, which don't pollute. Germany has also passed laws to try to achieve zero waste. That means Germans are recycling everything from soft-drink bottles to automobiles.

Changing genes may kill bad bugs

We may not need to spray pesticides on plants to kill harmful insects or funguses. Scientists are changing the genes of some plants (the process is called "genetic modification") so that the plants can make their own pesticides. Genetically modified cotton seeds are already being planted in India, and modified soybeans and other crops are being grown in the United States. Chili, potato, eggplant, rice, and cabbage seeds are being tested. Sounds good. A quick fix! But many scientists and others warn that genetic modification may affect other living things, including human beings, in ways we can't yet predict, ways which may be harmful.

DEFINITION, PLEASE!

Genes are the tiny managers in the cells of each living thing that decide what characteristics it will have. Before you were born, genes decided the shape of your nose and the color of your eyes. Decisions, decisions!

Inside a California granary, an adult barn owl perches high up on a rafter. When night falls, she will use her excellent hearing, big eyes, and deadly talons to capture juicy mice and rats. (Courtesy of The Hungry Owl Project)

Skip the Poison

The Hungry Owl Project (HOP) in California wants to reduce the need for pesticides and rodenticides, so it teaches people about the importance of owls as natural predators. The average-sized family of seven owls eats 5,000 rodents in one three-month breeding season! Yet not enough of the owls' habitat is being conserved. One kind of owl, the barn owl, likes to nest in barns and silos or in tree cavities. Because we don't have as many farms or big old trees as we used to, HOP helps kids make boxes that owls can nest in.

When HOP is invited to classes, scout troops, and clubs, the kids are shown a video about barn owls. They learn that the barn owl's natural hunting grounds are disappearing and how we can try to preserve the essential wild hedges and rough grasslands. The kids might even get to meet a great horned owl that HOP brings from a wildlife refuge. Under adult supervision, the kids get down to work making owl boxes. HOP sells these

Kids from the Marin Conservation Corps use power tools to build owl boxes, which then get a coat of stain to protect the wood. (Courtesy of The Hungry Owl Project)

DID YOU KNOW?

If you find an owl in danger or fallen from a nest, the best way you can help is by getting it into the hands of a person or organization licensed to treat wildlife. In the meantime, put a cardboard box over it or put it in a quiet place (wear heavy gloves!) and absolutely do not feed it anything. And remember, in the United States it is illegal for you to keep a bird of prey, even if you mean to release it later.

The kids show off their construction project—enough boxes to house six families of owls, with babies like the ones on the right. (Courtesy of The Hungry Owl Project)

nesting boxes to ranches, granaries, and vineyards that promise not to use rat poison. The money HOP earns goes toward buying supplies for more owl boxes and toward programs for teaching more kids about owls.

The renowned conservationist Jane Goodall (see chapter 10) believes strongly in how important kids are to helping animals that in turn help the earth. As she says, "Owls are vanishing from so many parts of their historic range. As one example, the barn owls whose haunting voices thrilled my childhood nights are gone. That is why the Hungry Owl Project is a much needed and very important initiative. I hope that every bird lover, every nature lover, will support it. Let us ensure that these marvelous birds, with their huge eyes and silent flight, will be around to bring magic to the night long after we are gone. Their future lies in our hands."

Blind and helpless when they hatch out of their eggs, these young barn owls will eventually lose their white baby fluff for speckled brown feathers. By the time they are two months old, they will fly out of the nest on quietly powerful wings and into the night. (Courtesy of The Hungry Owl Project)

A Mouse in the House: Biological Controls

You see a plump, scurrying body and then a flash of long tail disappearing under the couch. You jump on the couch and yell, "Yikes! There's a mouse in the house. Get the rat poison!"

Farmers have an even worse problem than yours. They have to deal with huge numbers of field mice and other rodents who eat their crops. And most farmers also yell, "Get the rat poison!" But rat poison, besides killing the rodents, harms humans, small animals, and birds. It, and other chemical pesticides, often mess up the natural balance of soil, bacteria, plants, insects, animals, and birds in our fields.

So what to do? Scientists and biologists are working to develop the natural enemies of the pesky little animals that eat our corn, alfalfa, and other crops. One of those scientists, Yossi Leshem (read about him in chapter 10), and his coworkers teach farmers how to build box nests for barn owls—whose favorite food is field mice. And they plan a careful balance of biologically safe pesticides to use along with the owls when necessary. The owl, with its sharp talons, large eyes, and head that swivels in almost a full circle, floats soundlessly over the fields and orchards at night and hunts mice to feed its hungry nestlings. The happy result for us is a pest-free, chemical-free environment.

If you're still standing on the couch, don't wait for a barn owl to float in and rescue you. Bait a box trap with peanut butter or cheese, wait for the trap's door to snap shut behind the hungry mouse, and then carry him off and free him in an empty field. If there's an owl on the prowl the mouse will soon know it.

BOBBI ANGELL

These lovely poppies were drawn by the botanical artist Bobbi Angell. The flowers come in many varieties with different petal shapes and colors ranging from pure white to candy pink and from orangey red to deep purple. In the United States, it's illegal for individuals to grow poppies that can be used for making drugs. (Making poppy-seed cookies is still okay.)

Plant Medicines

The yucky green mold you cut off a spoiled orange could help cure an illness some day. Scientists turned a mold like that into penicillin, which now saves people's lives. A pretty garden flower called foxglove provides digitalis, a medicine for heart patients. Beautiful poppies are the source of medicines like codeine and morphine, which lessen people's pain and help them to sleep. Your eye doctor uses atropine, from a plant of the potato family, to widen the pupil of your eye during an eye exam. And curare, a plant poison smeared on arrow tips by jungle hunters, was once used to relax a patient's muscles during surgery.

So the seeds, fruits, leaves, bark, and juice from hundreds of plants from the jungles, forests, and deserts of the earth are being used to help people. Many other plants haven't been discovered and studied yet. Can you imagine what cures we may be losing as we chop down more and more of the wild places of the earth?

Looking Backward and Forward

So many problems in just a quick look at Mr/Ms Earth's air, water, land, and growing human population. It almost feels as though we were better off a few hundred thousand years ago, when the air was clean and fresh, and the water was full of healthy fish. There was plenty of elbow room for us and the other animals, and giant forests shaded the world.

On the other hand, the first humans had to fight off cave bears and other giant predators with small, stone knives. And those first humans froze in the winter and roasted in the summer. When the snow fell and the streams iced over, people had to huddle close for warmth and hoard their meager baskets of wild grains, nuts, roots, dried berries, and meat, so they wouldn't die from hunger.

That doesn't sound good. Let's not go back there. But if we humans are so smart, why can't we find a way to have it all—a clean, beautiful Earth and a comfortable, enjoyable way of life? Wouldn't that fit in with the Bible's commandment to till the earth and also to take care of it?

Here's another question. Where do the other creatures of the earth fit in? This chapter was mostly about ourselves and how we used and abused our Earth. In the next chapter let's talk about what's happening to other living things that, like us, are part of the earth's inter-connected community.

A BIODEGRADABLE TRASH TEST

We're making more trash and garbage each year. Most of it ends up in landfills or gets burned in incinerators. Both solutions pollute our Earth. But we can improve things by separating out whatever is biodegradable and helping to turn that into good soil.

Which parts of our trash are biodegradable? This test will give you the answer.

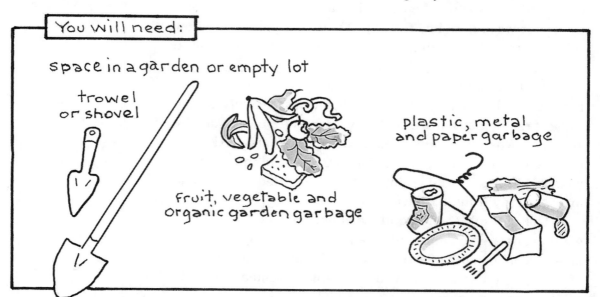

You will need:

space in a garden or empty lot

trowel or shovel

fruit, vegetable and organic garden garbage

plastic, metal and paper garbage

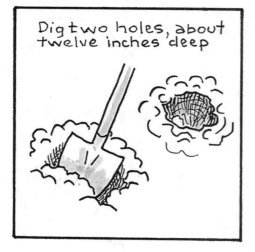

Dig two holes, about twelve inches deep

Put fruit, vegetable and garden waste in one hole and fill it with earth. Put plastic, metal and paper waste in the other hole and fill it with earth.

Be sure to ask permission before you start to dig the holes. If there's no rain in the next week or two, water the holes once or twice. Uncover both holes in a month and see what's happened.

What's Happening to the Animals?

Holy Animals

Once people used to worship animals. The Egyptians believed that cats were holy. They also worshipped a bull called Apis. Before American Indians would eat a deer or other game they had hunted, they would thank the spirit of the animal for providing them with food. Even the ancient Israelites, when they were alone and scared in the desert of the Sinai, made a calf out of gold that they thought would protect them. And later when there was a Temple in Jerusalem, the observance of Rosh Hashanah included sending a goat off into the desert—to carry away all of the Jews' sins. That poor goat was the original scapegoat! (Today we use the term "scapegoat" for a person or thing that is unfairly blamed for all kinds of problems.) Animals or birds were also brought to the Temple as sacrifices or gifts to God,

Fifteen thousand years ago, deep inside a dark cave lit only by a sputtering torch, an artist worked to create perfect images of bison and horses. It was cold outside. Europe was frozen in an ice age. The artist and his people trapped small animals for food. If they were lucky they found the carcass of a bison or a horse to eat. Maybe by drawing a picture of the bison, the artist was calling the spirit of the bison to come and feed the tribe. We'll never know. But we can be sure that the animals the artist painted were very important to him and his tribe, just as animals are for us today.

along with the fruits of the farmers' fields and orchards. Whether people prayed to animals, shared them with their gods, or just plain ate them, people throughout the ages respected animals and realized they were our partners in the world.

*I*n chapter 3 there were suggestions for pet care that were derived from Jewish religious laws and customs. There were also lots of questions, such as:

- Should we say a prayer over the grave of a beloved pet?

- Is it right to ask a rabbi to bless a new pet or to say *ha-gomel*, a prayer of thanks to God, for a pet that was nearly run over or that just recovered from a serious illness?

- What should you do if your pet has a litter of kittens or puppies that you can't keep and nobody wants to adopt?

- Is it right to ask your vet to euthanize ("put to sleep") a pet who is hopelessly sick or in pain?

It's much easier to ask these questions than to find answers in Jewish traditions because for many, many years people (Jewish and non-Jewish) didn't have pets. They had livestock, and they used animals to carry loads or pull wagons or plows, or for food. But as far as we know, nobody sat around petting animals or playing a game of Frisbee with them. So in Jewish law and custom there are plenty of rules for fairness and good care of work animals, but no rules about pets. Our rabbis now must search and think carefully as they go back to Jewish law to find answers to the new questions.

Pet Questions with Answers

Even a big, strong animal like a horse needs care. Sophie is "untacking" Termie (taking off his saddle and bridle), while Hannah gets ready to groom Tasha. The girls brush and wipe down their horses after every ride. (Photo by Bill Buckley. Courtesy of Epona Equine)

Today meat, chicken, and fish are sold in the supermarket, neatly ground or cut up and packed in smell-proof, plastic-wrapped trays—no hair or feathers, no scales or skin. There's not much indication of "animal." It's just packaged food to throw in the shopping cart. When people were closer to fishing or farming, or raised chickens in the backyard, they were better able to see animals as our partners in the world. We may not see them or think of them at all now, unless we have pets.

And pets are a good place to start thinking about the animals in our world. They're not independent like wild animals. They need us to feed them, play with them, make sure they get shots, and give them space to run around. Those aren't tough responsibilities. After all, pets are friends. Dogs and cats are fun to play with, and warm and loving to hold or scratch behind the ears. Even slow-moving turtles or silky-soft hamsters are interesting to watch and help us learn about lives so different from our own.

Here are some questions and answers about pets, which came from various "Ask the rabbi" Web sites:

> **My cat had a litter of six kittens. Nobody wants them, and I have no room for them. Should I let them loose in a park or maybe have them "put to sleep"?**

You should find an animal shelter that will care for them until they can be adopted. And you must alter or spay your pet so that it will have no new litters. Jewish tradition is against sterilizing an animal, but in this case, when you want to prevent suffering for future litters of unwanted kittens, it should be permitted.

A tragedy occurred. My cousin and his beloved dog were killed in an auto accident. Can they be buried side by side in a Jewish cemetery?

In Jewish tradition there is a distinction between animals and humans. We may love our pets, trust them, and feel that they are our friends. And we may miss them terribly when they die. But we don't see them as equal to humans, so as Jews, we don't bury them in our cemeteries. A Jewish cemetery is the final resting place of human beings, for whom this place of honor is reserved.

It's not just kittens, but also grownup cats, that are waiting in animal shelters for new homes. Patchwork hopes a boy or girl will give her lots of love, not to mention tuna fish. (Courtesy of the ASPCA)

When my rabbit dies, may I say *Kaddish*, the prayer we say at Jewish funerals?

Kaddish is a prayer praising God. It's a religious expression used to memorialize family members and others to whom we've been close. As much as you may love your pet, reciting *Kaddish* isn't an appropriate way to remember it. Instead you can plan a ceremony where you tell stories about your pet and show photos, or perhaps bury your pet's favorite toys. And it would be a mitzvah (a good deed) to contribute money to an animal shelter in your community in honor of your pet.

Look at the size of those paws! This lucky puppy is on his way from the animal shelter to a new home, where we hope he'll grow up big, healthy, and strong. What name will the family give him? (Courtesy of the ASPCA)

My family is talking about having our very old dog "put to sleep." Do we have the right to do that?

Jewish tradition is against mercy killing. On the other hand, Jewish law forbids causing suffering to animals. So, if your pet is very sick or badly injured and can't be healed, you may take it to the vet to end its life as painlessly as possible.

These are the opinions of a few rabbis. Other rabbis and learned Jews may have other opinions. When you have a question about pets, it might help to talk the question over with your rabbi.

Wild Animals

The Bible tells us that Noah built an ark to float above the Great Flood that would drown the world. Before the waters rose, he brought aboard a pair of all living things on Earth. Thanks to Noah, his wife Naamah, and their children, who worked hard for 40 days and nights to keep their passengers happy, we have a wonderful variety, or biodiversity, of species on Earth today. Today many scientists believe that biodiversity is a result of the evolution of living things and their adaptation to their environments. Whether we thank Noah or evolution, we are grateful that billions of living things of all shapes, sizes, and colors busily eat and grow and reproduce in a connected chain of life on our planet. Trees give off oxygen, which makes it possible for all of us to breathe. Birds nest in the trees and eat insects. Insects and birds flit through the flowers spreading seeds and pollen that help new plants and trees to grow in farmers' fields and in the wild. From tiny to huge, we all connect to each other.

In the last 100–150 years people have been thoughtlessly ruining our world's biodiversity. We've sprayed pesticides over our fields to kill insects and rodents that were eating our crops. But birds and small animals that ate the poisoned insects and animals or the pesticide-covered crops got sick or died, too. In the United States pesticides kill 67 million birds a year. It's like a policeman on the street who fires his gun to stop a criminal but accidentally hits innocent bystanders. One innocent bystander was the bald eagle—the fierce, proud symbol of the United States. Eagles that ate small animals that were killed by the pesticide DDT began to lay eggs with very soft shells. Many of the baby eagles weren't protected by their shells and died before they hatched. Today, with the banning of DDT, the eagle population is growing again.

DEFINITION, PLEASE!

There are millions of different species of plants, animals, funguses, and microbes on our Earth. The variety of all their differences is called **biodiversity**. Every species affects every other species in some way, even if they're as different from each other as a huge elephant and a tiny snail. And we all need each other. As species disappear, we all become poorer.

We use chemical fertilizers to make our crops grow larger and produce more fruit in our orchards. But each heavy rain sends fertilizers and pesticides oozing off the fields and into the waterways. "Green algae"—aquatic plantlike organisms—love the fertilizer and grow to fill and clog the streams. The fish get hit twice, by the crowding algae and by the poisonous pesticides. Beds of bright coral (tiny sea animals with stoney textures) and many species of fish are being killed by water pollution. And many of the surviving

This elephant in Amboseli National Park in Kenya wants to protect her baby from all harm. Millions of elephants once roamed the entire continent of Africa. But people hunted them for their ivory tusks and also started building houses where the elephants needed to live. In the last century, the number of African elephants has declined drastically, down to one percent of the number there once were. (Photo by Roger Harris. Courtesy of junglephotos.com)

A sick, young whale was swept onto a beach in southern Israel. Naturalists tried to save its life but they failed. Inside the whale's stomach they found a tangle of plastic bags that the animal had swallowed. The bags had plugged up its stomach and caused it to starve to death. This also happens with sea turtles off the coast of New Jersey and to other sea creatures all over the world. Be sure to put garbage in trash cans! (Photo by Chaya M. Burstein)

fish are scooped up by fishing boats with nets as big as several football fields. Because of this massive killing, the fish population can't reproduce and fully replace itself.

Meanwhile, back on dry land wild animals are in trouble, too. Big jungle animals in Africa, Southeast Asia, and India are being overrun by the growing human population, as are thousands of other species of living things in the great Amazon rain forests of South America.

First We Mistreat and Then We Eat

Remember how the Bible tells us to till the earth and take care of it? And the laws of *Shabbat* warn us to let our work animals rest and give them the freedom to roam on their day off. We don't take these laws seriously anymore. Not even in Israel, the land of the Bible.

As we just read in chapter 7, the world's population is growing quickly. Some farmers and large corporations that raise animals are finding efficient ways to increase production, but they aren't thinking about compassion or kindness to living things.

DID YOU KNOW?

We like to think of animal farms as places where cows graze in green fields, and chickens have the run of the barnyard. But too many animals today are raised in vast, dark, overcrowded buildings people describe as "factory farms." These places are run by huge food companies, not by traditional farmers deeply connected to the land.

Most chickens are raised closely crowded together in big chicken houses. They become egg-laying machines sitting on wire mesh with their eggs and waste dropping to a moving belt underneath. Bright lights keep them awake so that they will keep laying eggs day and night.

Many cows are penned into separate narrow spaces in immense barns. They're fed and milked regularly so they make lots of milk, but they never enjoy sunlight or move around freely. Young calves are confined, too, so that they will not jump and run and play. Running would make their muscles strong, which would make their meat tough. The calves are slaughtered to make tender cuts of veal.

People do many other cruel things to animals. They force food down the throats of geese to make their livers grow large so that humans can enjoy a food called "goose liver pâté." And animals are used in experiments to test new medicines, cosmetics, and food products. The Talmud warns us that according to the principles of "don't destroy" and "mercy toward animals," we'd better have a very good reason to cause pain to a living creature. If it's to test a new medicine to cure illness—that's a good reason. If it's to develop a new surgical technique to save people's lives—that's a good reason. But if it's to find out whether a new brand of lipstick will irritate the skin, or if it's to provide perfect white fur for expensive coats by clubbing baby seals—are those good reasons?

Slowly, Hopefully, We're Changing Things

Not everything is getting worse and worse. Many people care about animals and about a balance of living things on our Earth, and they're trying to turn things around.

• DDT, one of the pesticides that kills many "innocent bystanders" and remains in the earth for decades without breaking down, is now illegal throughout much of the world.

- Many people are upset by the cruel ways that animals are raised for food. They are demanding that animals be allowed to live a more normal life. And some believe that the eggs, meat, and milk of naturally grown animals is healthier food. Today you can buy free-range eggs, laid by chickens who were free to peck and scratch and enjoy life while they were providing the ingredients for your breakfast omelet.

- Some people and countries work together to make our Earth healthier. In 1987, representatives of many countries met in Montreal, Canada, and agreed to stop using chemicals that destroy the earth's ozone layer. In Barcelona, Spain, in 1992 countries pledged to stop throwing industrial waste into the sea. And the Kyoto Protocol to limit global warming, which was initiated in 1992, has been signed by many nations and is slowly gaining support. That same year, in Rio de Janeiro, Brazil, representatives of many nations agreed to work to protect biodiversity on our planet. In 2002 another Earth summit was held in Johannesburg, South Africa. There are international efforts to clean up oil spills, to protect whales from being wiped out, to limit fishing, and to deal with many other problems.

- Naturalists all over the world are gathering the eggs of endangered species of birds, hatching and raising them in protected shelters, and then releasing the young birds to fly free when they're strong enough. Salmon hatchlings are raised in protected areas and then allowed to swim off into the ocean. (To find out more about salmon, read

DID YOU KNOW?

Jews who keep to a strictly kosher diet will eat meat only if the animal has been killed in a specific way described in the Talmud and later Jewish teachings. Intended to take the animal's life in a most humane and painless way, the work is done by a specially trained and equipped *shochet*, which means "ritual slaughterer." Observant Muslims use a somewhat similar method of ritual slaughter called *halal*.

DEFINITION, PLEASE!

Ozone is a rare gas. Most of the ozone layer, or ozonosphere, is found in a layer of the atmosphere that begins about eight miles above the earth (beyond the clouds) and extends up about 30 miles higher. This "stratospheric" ozone absorbs most of the sun's ultraviolet-B radiation that could harm plants and animals.

"Pigeon Creek Kids" in chapter 10.) In the United States buffalo herds are growing again, and wolves and other natural predators are being returned to national parks and wilderness areas. The naturalists who do this work are modern Noahs.

- Ten percent of the earth's lands have been set aside as national parks where animals live free. The United States led that parade in 1972 by establishing Yellowstone National Park (located mostly in Wyoming)—the first national park in the world. Today there are all kinds of parks ranging from Hawaii's Volcanoes National Park, with the bubbling, smoking Kilauea volcano, to Sareks National Park in Sweden, with evergreen forests and creeping glaciers. The volcanic island of St. John in the U.S. Virgin Islands is a tiny Garden of Eden, with its mountainous tropical jungle surrounded by white sand beaches and clear, blue-green seas.

The world's newest park is the huge Lope National Park in the central African country of Gabon. It's home to elephants, gorillas, crocodiles, leopards, chimpanzees, and birds like the emerald cuckoo, the rosy bee-eater, and the chocolate-backed kingfisher. Of course, there are some problems. Poachers sneak in to kill wild animals, and loggers keep cutting down trees in prohibited areas. The government is working to save the park by stopping these greedy people. And for hungry people who kill the animals to feed their families, or trap and sell them as the only way to earn a living, it is trying to find other occupations and sources of income.

Under the best circumstances, national parks are places where animals can survive safely in their habitats. And then human visitors get to enjoy the beautiful scenery and appreciate the biodiversity of God's creatures—big or small, fierce or gentle, fluffy or smooth, rough or slimy. Many families head to national parks when it's time for summer vacation.

A Walk in the Park

This family is enjoying a wonderful day in Yellowstone National Park. On the next four pages, look at what they might see up in the mountains, down in the valleys, in the rivers or woods, and—if they come back for a winter vacation—in the snow.

Bighorn sheep

Mountain goat

Pika

Wolverine

Desert canyon turtle

Grizzly bear

Yellow-bellied sapsucker

Yellow-bellied marmot

Praying mantis

Spider web on a sunflower

Badger

122

Mule deer

Mountain lion

Bison

Fox

Deer mouse

JOHN GOOD

Chipmunk

Snowshoe hare

BHB

Columbia spotted frog

SEAN NEILSEN

White pelican

BRYAN HARRY

Coyote

BRYAN HARRY

Homegrown

These girls are ready for fruit tasting at an Israeli farmers' market. One of them is sitting on a watermelon. Let's hope it doesn't break! (Photo by Albatross/Itamar Grinberg. Courtesy of Israel Ministry of Tourism)

Eden Trenor's market in Washington State brings farmers and townspeople together, and the food and flowers couldn't be better. (Photo by Deborah Nedelman)

Strawberries from Florida and tomatoes from Mexico are great treats in mid-winter. But they, and other out-of-season fruits and vegetables, use tons of fossil fuel to get from their farms to our supermarkets. Many people buy produce in "farmers' markets," where they hope the food sold has been grown locally or has been grown organically without chemical sprays and fertilizers. Some consumers are vegans. They don't eat animal products such as milk, cheese, eggs, and meat. With the guidance of nutrition experts, they can keep themselves well fed and healthy from nuts, beans, soybeans, and other foods of the earth.

There are also "natural food markets" in many cities that sell not only things to eat, but also recycled household paper and environmentally safe cleaning products, candles, soap, and cosmetics.

Eden Trenor runs a farmers' market in Mukilteo, Washington. Each Thursday afternoon from May to November, trucks rattle onto a grassy field near the ferry dock. The farmers unload their great wheels of home-made cheese, glorious flowers, fresh fruits, vegetables, and grains. They also bring eggs from free-range chickens, cuts of meat from cattle that were raised in fields (not factories), and ice-packed boxes of local salmon. Customers carrying string bags wander among the stalls. They stop and chat, enjoying each other's company—even when it's drizzling, which happens a lot in Mukilteo.

ECO-ACTIVITY · ECO-ACTIVITY

MAKING COMPOST

Dumping is still the major way of getting rid of trash, and we dump tons of it each day. If you have a garden, as much as one-third to one-half of that garbage doesn't have to be wasted. You can use vegetable peels, spoiled vegetables, apple cores, and other organic garbage from the kitchen. Add garden scraps, such as grass clippings and fallen leaves. Combine it all together to build a compost pile. (Don't use meat, bones, or other animal products because they'll attract dogs and cats to your pile.)

The pile will slowly decay into a crumbly, brown mixture. After a few months you can mix the compost with garden soil to feed your plants. You can also pile compost around plants and trees as mulch to keep the earth moist underneath.

Here's one way to compost:

1

At a garden or hardware store buy a composter – a large container with a lidded opening at the top – and another on the side and/or the front, near the ground.

2

Place the composter in the corner of the garden.

3

Dump in garden and kitchen waste each day. Keep a covered container on the kitchen counter near the sink to hold the waste till you can dump it. The compost should always be moist – so add a pail of water after a dry week.

ECO-ACTIVITY
ECO-ACTIVITY

4

About once every two weeks turn the pile with a garden fork or shovel to add air to to the mix. Oxygen in the air is used by the hardworking bacteria that are turning your garbage into plant food.

5

In 4-6 months you can open the side opening and dig out crumbly, dark compost, ready to use in the garden.

Here's a second way to compost:

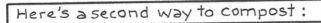

1

In a corner of the garden, place a circular pen of wire fencing. Use lightweight wire like chicken wire,

2

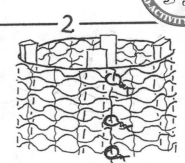

Hook the ends of the fencing together with wire so you can open it to turn or remove the compost.

3

Follow the instructions in steps 3-5 above.

Here's a third way:

1

In a corner of the garden, dig a shallow pit in the ground, about 2 feet in diameter.

2

Follow instructions in steps 3-5 above — and dig out crumbly compost in about six months.

Dirty Energy

Energy is what makes things work and makes things move. Without energy, we wouldn't have toasters, TV sets, computers, jet planes, lawn mowers, and other useful things. Most power today, even to generate electricity, comes from fossil fuels—oil, natural gas, and coal—which are pumped or dug out of the ground.

There are two big problems with fossil fuels. After we consume them, it takes millions of years for the earth to make more. And we are using up our supply of fossil fuels very quickly. The other thing is that fossil fuels are dirty.

They pollute the air when they're burned. Most of the world's air pollution is caused by excess carbon dioxide, nitrogen oxide, and other elements released as exhaust from power plants and from engines.

WHAT CAN WE DO ABOUT ENERGY POLLUTION?

We're trying to find efficient ways to make a kind of energy that won't pollute and won't get used up. It's called renewable energy, and it comes from the sun, the movement of water and wind, and the earth's internal heat. We have to catch the sun's power in solar collectors, harvest water power at waterfalls, dams, and in the ocean's tides, and catch the huge power of the wind with the turning blades of modern windmills. In Iceland, in the United States at Yellowstone Park, and in other parts of the world, the earth's deep internal heat boils up through cracks in the crust and gives us geothermal energy to heat houses and to push steam turbines in power plants.

Hundreds of windmill blades hum like a giant hive of bees. They're using the wind's power, which blows across hilltops near San Francisco, California, to turn a generator that makes electricity.
(Photo by Emanuel Ben David)

Splitting the nucleus of atoms, tiny bits of matter, is also a source of power. Nuclear power is produced in nuclear plants, and it's renewable and powerful. But accidental leakage from a nuclear plant can poison the land around it and kill or damage people and animals, as it did in the city of Chernobyl in the Ukraine in 1986. And there is an added problem. Even if there are no accidents, there's ongoing trouble with disposing of the "leftovers." Scientists haven't found a way to neutralize radioactive waste. It stays "hot" or dangerous for thousands of years. And no matter where it is stored, radioactive waste has to be safeguarded to keep it from being stolen by irresponsible people and used to make nuclear weapons.

So, getting back to the safe, nonpolluting, renewable fuels—they look like our best hope for a comfortable, livable future. Why aren't we using them? The reason is that they're still much more expensive than fuel from fossil materials.

This water-powered grain mill in Austria is only a tourist attraction today. But it shows that renewable, nonpolluting energy is an old story. Falling water from the wheel generated energy to turn the shaft, which then made the grinding stone go around. (Photo by Chaya M. Burstein)

A lot more money and thought has to be invested to develop efficient processes for using sun, water, wind, and geothermal spurces to create energy.

Even trash can be turned into energy. Much of the waste we discard every day (4¹/₂ pounds per average American!) can become fuel. Organic garbage, such as food scraps, can be transformed into methane gas, the main component of natural gas. Other trash can be burned to heat water that in turn generates steam-powered electricity or makes steam to heat buildings. Turning waste products into energy is a popular idea, although an expensive one.

Scientists and engineers have some other great ideas. For instance they'd like to build a space satellite that would sit above the earth's atmosphere and collect energy from the sun. Then it would transmit the energy to solar factories on the earth. Sounds like science fiction. It *is* science fiction today, when only 10 percent of the fuel we use comes from renewable sources. But if we put a lot of scientists and engineers to work figuring out ways to make renewable energy cheaper and more efficient, we'll surely find answers. Many things that were once science fiction became facts. (Do you know about the elaborate submarine *Nautilus* that Jules Verne dreamed up for the book *20,000 Leagues Under the Sea*?) Hey, think about it, maybe you'll be one of those scientists or engineers who comes up with an imaginative new idea for renewable energy!

Simple water wheels have evolved into rotary engines called turbines. Here is an inside view of the famous Hoover Dam while it was being built in the 1930s. Outside is the Colorado River, tamed to generate electric power for the modern age. In more recent years, engineers have begun to understand that large dams cause changes to the natural environment, like making it hard for salmon to swim upstream to their spawning area. They are trying to correct these problems and also design better dams for the future. (Courtesy of the U.S. Department of the Interior, Bureau of Reclamation)

HOW YOU AND I CAN USE ENERGY WISELY

Right now the best thing we can do to conserve energy is not to waste it. There are hundreds of ways to help. Here are a few:

- Turn off lights when we leave a room.

- In cold weather, keep the thermostat set to 68 degrees Fahrenheit or less and wear a sweater. In the summer, wear loose-fitting clothing and use window and room fans instead of so much air-conditioning.

- If we live in a house, ask the adults to save on heating and cooling costs by putting substantial insulation in the walls and roof.

- Our legs are clean, nonpolluting energy, so walk or bike to school, the store, or a friend's house whenever possible. And use buses and trains for longer trips. They carry more people and make less pollution per person than cars.

- When our families are car-shopping, think about Mr/Ms Earth and fuel conservation. Fuel-efficient, small cars are healthier for our air and our world than dinosaur-sized, gas-gulpers. Hybrid cars are now available, too. Hybrids use both gas and electricity for power and travel 50 miles on each gallon of gas. We could also remind the driver that the faster he or she drives above 55 miles per hour, the more gas is used per mile.

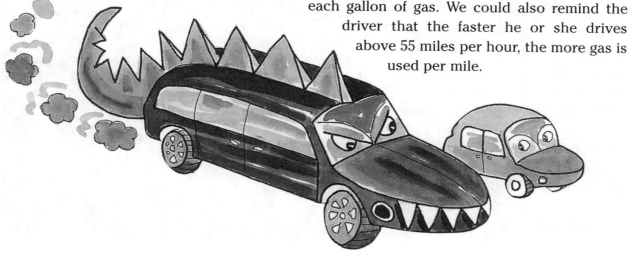

Solar collectors blink up at the sky from Israeli rooftops. They're working hard—collecting energy from the sun and using it to provide people with warm showers and clean dishes. See all those hot-water tanks on the roofs? (Courtesy of Israelimages.com)

- Ask about the possibility of putting a solar water heater on the roof of your house or apartment building. The collector panels use the sun to heat water—for free. In parts of the world that get little sun, solar heaters aren't currently as efficient as in places like Israel. But they are helping almost everywhere, even on roofs in drizzly Seattle, Washington.

Too Much Trash

We make so much trash and garbage that there's often no room near the cities to dump it. Some cities pile their trash into trucks or onto barges that travel miles to dump their loads in faraway, empty spaces. These may once have been a wetland full of birds or a green cow pasture. Slowly the garbage turns into a moldering mountain, a delicious home for flies and rats. When a garbage mountain gets so tall that the junk starts sliding down, cities dump earth on top of it and sprinkle that with grass seed. Then they start haulng their trash to another "empty" space.

WHAT CAN WE DO INSTEAD OF DUMPING?

- Some towns build incinerators to burn as much of the trash as is burnable. They put screens and traps on the tall incinerator chimneys to keep bits of rubbish from flying out. But unfortunately the screens can't stop all the polluting particles and gases from rising into the sky.

DID YOU KNOW?

One hundred years ago the biggest pollution problem in New York City was horse manure! Horse manure on shoes, on carriage wheels, clogging the sewers—it was everywhere. Thousands of horses pulled wagons, carriages, fire engines, and everything else on wheels. Well, at least we've solved that problem!

- The most environmentally friendly towns teach their citizens to separate their trash and garbage into several containers. One may hold organic waste like fruit and vegetable peels and grass clippings. Another may hold plastic bottles, metal cans, glass jars, broken toys, and plastic tableware. A third may hold newspapers, bags, and other paper goods. The town collects everything. It then dumps the organic waste into a giant compost pile. Air is injected into the pile, which heats up, ripens, and slowly turns into healthy soil and mulch for parks and gardens. The newspapers and other paper goods are mashed, chopped, bleached, and sifted through a screen. Finally the mash is spread in a sheet and dried. It leaves the recycling plant as new, usable paper. And the plastic or metal garbage is sorted and melted down or cut up to be used for new products.

- The best recycling isn't perfect. There's still stuff left over. But we'd better recycle because dumping won't solve the problem anymore. We're running out of dumping room!

HOW YOU AND I CAN CUT DOWN ON TRASH

- First of all, try to cut down on the amount of stuff we buy. Less buying means less throwing out.

- If our town has a recycling program, separate the items we put in the trash. And take empty cans and bottles back to the store, if the state has a deposit or recycling plan.

- Cut down on the use of one-time-only plastic bags, dishes, utensils, and cups. A large part of our trash is plastic, and it takes years to break down after it's buried in a garbage dump.

DID YOU KNOW?

Each ton of recycled paper saves 17 trees. Is your town recycling paper? Old paper gets a new life as bags, office stationery, toilet paper, and more.

- If we have a garden, build a compost pile for organic waste. The good bacteria in the pile will happily eat one-third to one-half of our garbage. (See how to compost at the end of chapter 8.)

- When we outgrow clothing, pass it on to other family members or friends, or bring it to a resale shop or homeless shelter. And when we're clothes shopping, we can check the thrift stores or resale shops. We'll be recycling and saving money at the same time.

You make streams gush forth in torrents,
They make their way between hills,
Giving drink to all the wild beasts.
The wild donkey slake their thirst.
The birds of the sky dwell beside them
And sink among the foliage.

Psalms 104:10–12

The Bible could have been describing the clean, sparkling water of this stream in northern Israel. There are still beautiful places to wade and swim in our world. Have fun! (Photo by Bernard Goobich)

Dirty Water

Take a long, slow drink of water from your sink tap. Do you taste the chlorine? Most of our water is treated with chlorine or other chemicals to kill harmful bacteria. That's why many people buy bottled water, which they hope comes from clear, clean, natural springs that don't need purifiers. Most of the world's people can't afford bottled water, and their tap water (for those who even have running water) is getting dirtier each day. As we learned in chapter 6, there's plenty of fresh water in the world. But as more and more people use that water, it's getting loaded with chemicals and soap and with waste from factories, homes, and farm fields. Even the rainwater that runs across parking lots and down streets picks up harmful substances. Untreated wastewater pollutes rivers, lakes, and oceans, or filters down through the earth to pollute underground water sources.

WHAT CAN WE DO ABOUT DIRTY WATER?

Some cities have plants for treating (separating and cleaning) wastewater. This process partly solves the problem of dirty water. First, smelly gases are removed by spraying the water into the air. Then the water is recaptured and sent to big tanks or ponds, where it is filtered more to get out the grit, sludge, and bacteria. That makes it clean enough to be used on farms and in industrial plants. Some of the water may be purified even more, so that it's clean enough to use in our kitchens. But unfortunately, most of the world is not rich enough (or, too often, not caring enough) to build these expensive wastewater treatment plants. The wastewater just gets dumped on the ground to be purified naturally as it filters through the earth. But today much of the water is so dirty that when it seeps down it pollutes our underground water resources. If it flows into lakes and oceans, it pollutes them, too.

DID YOU KNOW?

Another way to provide fresh water is "desalinization." In some dry parts of the world like Saudi Arabia and Kuwait, the salt is taken out of sea water so that it can be used for farming, cooking, and drinking.

This wastewater treatment plant processes about one-third of the drinking water consumed each day by the people of Atlanta, Georgia. If your eyes can see the tiny-looking cars in the parking lot and the truck on the highway, you'll have an idea of how big the ponds and tanks are. (Courtesy of the U.S. Geological Survey)

HOW YOU AND I CAN SAVE WATER

- Don't waste. Take a shower instead of a bath. Showers take only two-thirds as much water. Don't let the water run while we're brushing our teeth or washing the dishes. Turn it on to soap up, then turn it off until it's time to rinse.

- When we need a new toilet, ask our families to consider a "dual-flush" tank with two handles, one for a light flush and one for a heavy flush. Many homes already have these in Israel and Australia. Almost half of our household water is spent flushing the toilet.

- If we have a garden, think about using "drip irrigation." A special soaker hose drips water exactly where it's needed. That's better than spraying (some of that water evaporates in the air) or sprinkling (some of that water ends up on plants that don't need it).

These goats roam the hillside pastures in Switzerland. They nibble here and there, rest a little, nibble again, and produce delicious milk for making wonderful cheese. (Photo by Chaya M. Burstein)

DEFINITION, PLEASE!

Hybrid used to just mean the offspring of two different kinds of plants or animals. A nectarine is a hybrid—a cross between a peach and a plum. And a mule is a cross between a horse and a donkey. Now the word hybrid can also describe a vehicle that runs on two different sources of power.

- Suggest to your family members that they buy organically grown food. Or, think about growing your own food organically in your garden or in a community lot. Here are some of the pros and cons to discuss:

Pro:

1. There's less soil and water pollution with organically grown crops than with chemically grown.

2. The food may be healthier.

3. Eggs, chickens, and dairy and meat products come from animals that live in a natural environment. Organically grown food helps us to follow the important tradition of *tzaar baalei chaim*, kindness to animals.

Con:

1. Organically grown foods may not be available in your neighborhood.

2. They're usually more expensive. And because they don't have preservatives, they might spoil faster.

3. They may not look as perfect as produce grown with chemicals.

The city of Portland, Oregon, is the U.S. leader in building new electric trolley lines. This one is free to ride within a large portion of the city. (Courtesy of Portland Streetcar Company)

Help from Higher up

We've talked about the problems of our Earth and we've thought about what we ourselves can do to improve the environment. But there are so many problems that have to be handled from higher up, so let's push really hard to get help for Mr/Ms Earth. Here's what we can ask our city, state, and national governments to do:

- Spend more money on building and maintaining railroads, bus lines, and other mass transportation. Once upon a time, before so many American families owned two or three cars, small and large towns in most of the United States were connected by rail and trolley lines. To help lower the amount of air pollution caused by car and truck exhaust, we need to rebuild our mass transit systems.

- Invest our country's tax dollars in finding efficient ways to use renewable sources of energy, such as wind, sun, and water.

- Require separation and recycling of trash and build treatment plants for wastewater and discarded materials. Local government officials sometimes complain that recycling is expensive. We must convince them to add up the cost of trash disposal and cleanups of polluted air, water, and earth. Then subtract that cost from the cost of recycling, because recycling will eliminate a lot of disposal and cleanup costs.

DID YOU KNOW?

Hybrid cars are becoming popular. They run on electricity and gasoline. Seattle, Washington, even has hybrid buses—diesel-electrics. They draw electric power from overhead wires and run on diesel fuel when they're away from the wires.

- Buy energy-efficient hybrid or natural-gas vehicles when it's time for your government to replace its official cars and trucks.

- Cooperate with international efforts to preserve forests and wildlife, to stop global warming, and to reduce pollution of water, land, and air.

If you think of more ideas, add them to the list. And then send a letter to your town, state, or federal government representative. It is good to make your letter short, so pick one problem, explain it, and describe what you think needs to be done. You might even include a photo of yourself or the issue you are discussing. Sign the letter and include your return address so you can get an answer. Regular mail gets the most personal attention, but e-mail and fax are good, too.

As you probably know, in the United States government we have a president, two senators representing each state, and one congressperson (also called a U.S. representative) for each congressional district. Besides a governor, each state has a legislature with senators and representatives (some states have "assembly members"), who have offices both in your district and and in the state capital. The town, city, or county where you live has someone like a mayor or a commissioner and a town council who

TZEDAKAH FOR MR/MS EARTH

The Hebrew word tzedakah means righteousness or justice, and it feels right and just to treat Mr/Ms Earth as generously as he/she has treated us. So if some of the eco-groups listed in this chapter look good to you, think of ways to help their work. You could raise money by baking cookies, putting them in a decorated "Save the Earth" bag (biodegradable, please) and selling them at your community center. Or you could raise money by washing cars (to save water use a pail and a brush instead of the hose). Or you could contribute some of your birthday or Hanukkah gift money.

run the show. Use the Internet to find out the names of your elected officials.

Here are examples of how you would address various envelopes:

- The President
  The White House
  Washington, D.C. 20500

- The Honorable
  (governor's name)
  State Capital Building
  (name of your state
  capital, state, and
  zip code)

- The Honorable
  (mayor's name)
  City Hall
  (name of your city,
  state, and zip code)

- The Honorable
  (U.S. senator's name)
  U.S. Senate
  Washington, D.C. 20510

- The Honorable
  (U.S. representative's
  name)
  U.S. House of
  Representatives
  Washington, D.C. 20515

- The Honorable
  (state senator's name)
  State Legislature Building
  (name of your state
  capital, state, and
  zip code)

- The Honorable (state
  representative's name)
  State Legislature Building
  (name of your state
  capital, state, and
  zip code)

Michaela (on the left) and Sakshi plant flowers at their school's "Garden of Hope" in Columbia, Maryland. (Courtesy of The Jane Goodall Institute)

Eco-groups

Some people work together as groups to keep our Earth healthy. That way they may have more influence than each of us separately. You can explore the groups listed below on the Internet. (Find additional interesting groups by searching under words like "environment" or related topics that interest you.)

- American Society for the Prevention of Cruelty to Animals (ASPCA)

- Coalition on the Environment and Jewish Life (COEJL)

- Friends of the Earth

- Greenpeace International

- National Wildlife Federation

- Roots & Shoots (see Jane Goodall in chapter 10)

- Sierra Club

- Society for the Protection of Nature in Israel (SPNI)

- The Nature Conservancy

- Wildlife Conservation Society

Nicholas (on the left) and Derek know that Geronimo, a ring-necked dove, wants to be held securely, but gently, with a hand placed under his feet. (Photo by Michael J. Boorse. Courtesy of Germantown Friends School)

The Environmental Protection Agency (EPA) is a U.S. government agency that provides information that can help you make your family's home, garden, and car friendlier to the environment. It even has an Environmental Kids Club that you can find on the Internet.

You might be able to start or join a local eco-group. At the nature-loving Germantown Friends School, in Philadelphia, kids can participate in the Animal Care Club, which is responsible for the welfare of all the science-room animals. Volunteer fourth- and fifth-grade students, working in two-week shifts, arrive a half-hour before school starts. They wash bowls, clean and repaper cages, and cut up food for the animals. Learning the nature and habits of their charges, the kids discover that Sophie, a $2\frac{1}{2}$-foot-long ball python, swallows a mouse for breakfast. Two turtles, both of them red-eared sliders, slurp up earthworms like they were spaghetti. Geronimo, a ring-necked dove, never stops cooing and burbling—especially during school tests. It's worth getting up early for fun like this! And when school lets out in June, every kid hopes to be chosen to take an animal home for summer care. How would you like to "pet-sit" a blue-tongued skink—a lizard native to Australia?

PLANT A TASTY GARDEN, OUTDOORS OR IN

For fun, for the best-tasting vegetables, for the amazement of seeing seeds turn into plants . . .

PLANT A VEGETABLE GARDEN!

A vegetable garden needs good soil, water, sunlight, warmth, enough space between plants, and fertilizer. For a small, first-time garden, a 10-foot square of land is good.

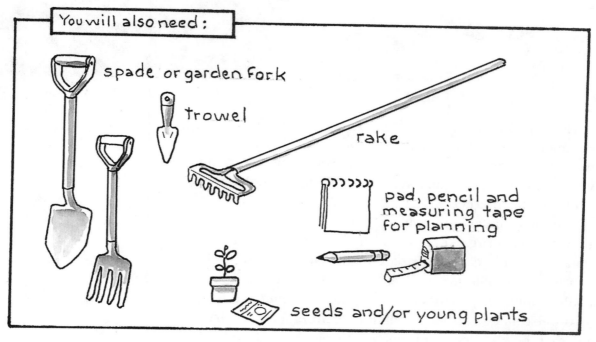

You will also need:

spade or garden fork

trowel

rake

pad, pencil and measuring tape for planning

seeds and/or young plants

1. Lay out the boundary of your plot with rocks, strings, or boards.

2. Decide which vegetables to plant. Radishes, carrots, lettuce, green peppers, and tomatoes make a pleasing group. Look at the seed packets to see how much space to leave between plants. Make a drawing to plan your layout.

3. Prepare the soil. Good garden soil is made up of tiny animals and plants, water, air, minerals, and organic materials. If your soil is crumbly and loose it's probably okay, but add some compost anyhow. If it's hard and clumpy it may have too much clay, so mix in peat moss and/or compost. Dig and turn the soil about 12 inches deep. Remove stones, break up clumps, and rake it smooth.

4. Follow the plan you've drawn and make grooves in the soil to mark where you'll put the seeds. For tomatoes and green peppers, you may want to buy young plants at the garden shop instead of planting seeds. That would give these warmth-loving plants a head start on the growing season. Other vegetables—like radishes, carrots, and lettuce—will grow well from the seeds.

If your plants are happy then, unfortunately, the weeds will be happy too. Yank 'em out!

5. Plant the seeds according to directions on the packet—and the young plants according to advice from the garden shop. Press the earth down firmly over the seeds and around the plants. Water lightly each day until the seedlings poke up.

6. When seedlings begin to come up, thin them as directed on the seed packet.

7. Fertilize your plants once or twice during the growing season.

8. Water the garden twice a week, or more often if it seems dry. And, hey—be patient and keep watering—seeds and plants can't be rushed!

If you have no land for a garden, or if you want to use your patio or balcony, try "container gardening." Rafael planted this geranium in a clay pot when it was only a few inches tall. With lots of sun and watering (plus two years time), it now has nine beautiful blooms. (Photo by Janet Greenstein Potter)

ECO-ACTIVITY

Here's a suggestion for a 10-foot-square plot containing five kinds of vegetables.

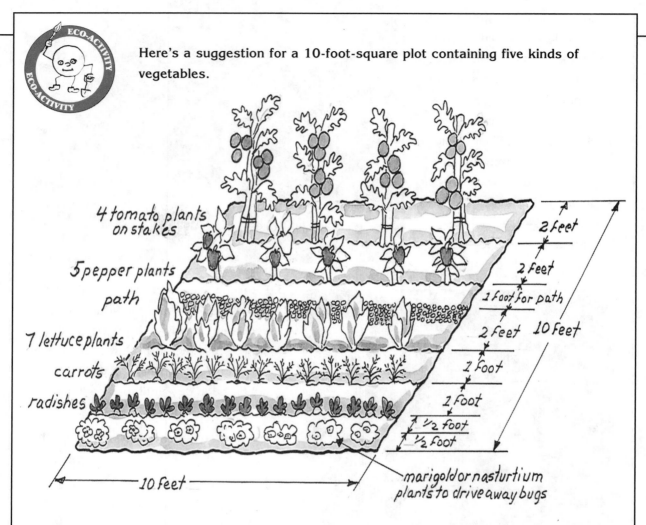

4 tomato plants on stakes

5 pepper plants

path

7 lettuce plants

carrots

radishes

2 feet

2 feet

1 foot for path

2 feet

1 foot

1 foot

½ foot

½ foot

10 feet

10 feet

marigold or nasturtium plants to drive away bugs

Some hints for your vegetable garden:

• Leave room for a path so you can weed easily.

• If your soil is really hard and rocky, build a frame of boards, brick, or block about one-foot high and fill it with garden soil.

• Put grass clippings or dry leaves around your plants as mulch. This will help keep them from drying out between waterings and slow the growth of weeds.

• Plant marigolds here and there among your vegetables. Bugs hate the smell of those flowers.

PLANT A WINDOWSILL GARDEN!

If you can't plant an outdoor garden, plant some salad herbs on a sunny windowsill. You could plant parsley for salads and soups. Or garlic for salads, hamburgers, soups, lasagna, etc. Or chives for salads, soups, and scrambled eggs. Or radishes for salads—and for the fun of watching them grow so quickly.

You will need:

- Seeds and a garlic bulb

- Planter box or several large flower pots

- Enough potting soil to fill the pots or box

- An old soup spoon

Here's what to do:

Parsley

Soak the seeds in water overnight. Plant in the potting soil as directed on the seed packet. Keep the soil moist.

Garlic

Buy a garlic bulb in the food store. Pull it apart into separate cloves. Plant the cloves about two inches deep and about two inches apart. You can snip off leaves to flavor salads when they grow about four inches tall. Or you can let each clove grow into a bulb in about three months. Keep moist.

Chives

Plant the seeds as directed on the seed packet. Snip the leaves as they grow, to flavor salads. A big plus—chive plants have pretty, purple flowers. Keep moist.

Radishes

Plant as directed on the packet. Pull up when the red radish top pokes out of the soil and seems about three-quarters of an inch in diameter. The greens are healthy in salads, too.

151

10 Eco-heroes

New plants push up in the spring and we wonder . . . how do they know when to sprout? Flocks of migrating birds sweep past, high in the sky. Again we wonder . . . how do they know where to go, and when to go? Will they be able to find their way back? Birds, plants, flowers—so many amazing, precious things in this world. But as we learned in earlier chapters, some of them are disappearing. Our human activities are killing them.

A lot of us say, "Tch, tch, tch. That's a pity." But some people say, "That's terrible and it has to be stopped!" And then they do something to change the situation.

The Bible warns us to take care of our wonderful Earth. People of all races and religions are taking that warning very seriously. They risk their safety, health, and even their lives for the earth. They are eco-heroes. Here are a few of their stories. There are many more.

Aaron Aaronson

(b. 1876 – d. 1919)

Sometimes Aaron felt like he was being pulled apart. Part of him was a botanist, a plant detective. And part of him was a fighter for freedom and independence for the Jewish people.

He loved to strap on his backpack and sneak out of the house in the quiet, early morning without waking his family. As the sun rose he'd be climbing over the dew-covered cliffs and hills of the Galilee in northern Palestine where he lived. Like many other botanists at that time, he was searching for the earliest wheat plant in the world—"emmer" wheat. It was the wheat that the first humans had discovered and eaten. If he could find this wild great-granddaddy of all modern wheat, he could use it to develop new, stronger, and richer strains of wheat. The tough new strains would be able to thrive in cold, wet winters and could feed more people.

Aaron's hometown was Zichron Yaacov, built on a mountain ridge above the shore of the Mediterranean. As he climbed he

DEFINITION, PLEASE!

Zion is one of the biblical names for the ancient walled city of Jerusalem and the Temple Mount where the First and Second Temples were located. It's also a name for ancient Israel.

would look down to the sea, where Turkish warships patrolled the shore. He hated them! The Turks were the enemy of his people. Aaron's parents had brought him to Palestine when he was six years old. They were Zionists, which means they dreamed of building a homeland for the Jews in their ancient land, Israel, called Palestine by numerous conquerors. But the Turks, who were the lords of the land, would never allow a Jewish homeland on their territory. They harassed the Jewish settlers constantly.

One morning in 1906, Aaron finally tracked down the wild wheat. At the oasis of Jericho, the cradle of agriculture, he found wild barley and two ancient forms of wheat. With trembling hands he examined the plants and carefully tucked samples into his backpack. He couldn't wait to get home and write the description of his finds. There would be scientific

papers to write, and articles and experiments to be carried out. So much good work. What an exciting time! But as he hurried home, he saw the Turkish ships still patrolling far below on the sea, like jackals circling a flock of sheep. His happiness faded.

A few years later the First World War began. Many countries were at war, including Great Britain, which was fighting the Turks for control of Palestine and the whole Middle East. "We promise to encourage the Jews to build a homeland in Palestine," the British told the Jews of the world. The promise hit the Aaronson family and the other Jews of Palestine like a jolt of electricity! Here was their chance for freedom. They desperately wanted the British to win the war.

Aaron pushed aside his papers on botany, and his bags and boxes of seeds and plant samples. Together, he and his brothers and his sister Sarah organized a spy ring that gathered information and passed it on to the British forces. For a while they succeeded in delivering messages to a British boat, right under the noses of the Turks. But then Sarah was caught when a message she sent by carrier pigeon was intercepted. The Turks tortured her to get information about her comrades in the spy ring. She kept silent, but the pain became unbearable. When she was left alone for a moment, she pulled out a gun that she had hidden and killed herself. Now Aaron's struggle for freedom was sealed in blood—the blood of his sister and of other friends.

The war finally ended. Aaron continued both of his important jobs—his work in botany and his struggle for a Jewish homeland. But he didn't get a chance to finish either of them. On his way to Paris for a post-war conference, where he was to argue for the founding of a Jewish homeland, Aaron died in a mysterious plane accident over the English Channel.

"**Y**ou wouldn't believe it, Rachel. I was standing at the sink washing dishes. I looked out the window and just then this robin dropped out of the sky—dead! Right in front of me! The spray from the mosquito-killing plane poisoned it. I'm sure of it."

Rachel Carson received this letter from a friend in the early 1960s. It was a time when scientists had started making powerful new chemicals to kill the bugs and funguses that harm farm crops. Farmers were enthusiastically spraying the

Rachel Carson

(b. 1907 – d. 1964)

DEFINITION, PLEASE!

A branch of biology, **botany** is the scientific study of plants—how they evolved, how they live, and what they can do for the world.

new chemicals on their crops from crop-dusting planes, tractors, and trucks. Later we would learn that these bug-killing chemicals (call insecticides) can make people sick. Back then, it seemed that only birds were affected. And farmers thought that tons of perfect apples, beans, and lettuce were worth the cost of a few dead birds.

Rachel, who grew up in a Pennsylvania river town, was a biologist. She studied living things, and she loved them—from squiggly squid to tiny, lost kittens. But the creatures of the ocean interested her most of all. She walked along the shore picking up fascinating sea animals. And she plunged deep into the sea in heavy boots and a diving helmet to explore the sea bottom. But Rachel also brought home injured dogs, cared for stray cats, and put back into the sea the creatures she had taken out briefly to study.

Her friend's letter upset Rachel. She had already written a few books about the sea, but now she decided to turn back to the land and see what was happening. And she found that sprays were killing the birds. How terrible it would be if all the birds died, she thought. What if spring came with the first crocus sparkling under the bushes and soft leaves uncurling on branches, but there were no bird sounds? What if spring-time tiptoed in silently—if there were no happy chirping to welcome it? And if birds were killed by the poisons, other creatures would eventually die too. Even people.

Rachel sat down and wrote a book called *Silent Spring*. She warned everyone that chemical insecticides were dangerous and were damaging to birds and all other living things. What an explosion that book caused!

DID YOU KNOW?

For many years, the biologist Rachel Carson worked at the U.S. Fish and Wildlife Service, which today manages more than 500 wildlife refuges. One of the refuges—on the southern coast of Maine—was renamed in Rachel's honor after her death. The Rachel Carson Wildlife Refuge and nearby lands provide food and habitat for many species of animals, such as moose, harbor seals, river otters, beavers, and more than 250 kinds of birds.

"Carson's nothing but a weepy cat-lover, dog-lover, bird-lover. She doesn't care about people at all!"

"She's totally unrealistic and impractical!"

"Carson is emotional and unbalanced!"

Rachel was verbally attacked by farmers, chemical companies, doctors, and government officials. But she would not be quiet. She kept writing, studying, and speaking, and finally testified before Congress to demand new laws that would protect human beings and the environment.

Silent Spring and brave Rachel Carson turned people around. We began to realize that we weren't all-powerful lords of the earth, but partners linked together in a chain of existence. What harms one may harm all.

Pete Seeger

(b. 1919 –)

Skinny Pete Seeger with his graying beard and floppy tennis hat strummed his banjo and sang verse after verse. And the kids and grownups sprawled on the deck of the sloop *Clearwater* sang along with him. The sails billowed and thumped in the breeze and the waves slapped at the hull, as the *Clearwater* carried her message up and down New York State's Hudson River.

> *Come along with me*
> *Upon this broad, old river*
> *And we will see*
> *What we can do.*
> *For when we work together*
> *In all kinds of weather*
> *There's no telling what the*
> *power of the people*
> *And the river can do.*

—from "Broad Old River"
music and words by Pete Seeger

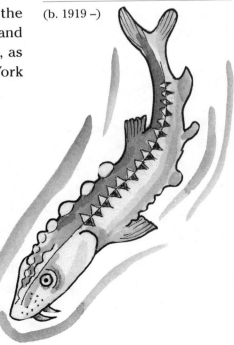

The river was dying. The sturgeon that had leaped, gleaming, from the current were gone. The shellfish that had fed the Indians were gone. Towns and factories along the river were dumping waste-water, and boats moving upstream pushed through garbage and toilet paper.

The *Clearwater* tied up at every dock, and people came down to listen. Pete Seeger strummed his banjo and sang funny songs like "This Old Car" and sad songs like "Where Have All the Flowers Gone?" Then he passed his banjo case around so that people could drop in money to carry on the fight to clean up the river.

It was hard work. But Pete Seeger was used to hard work. He had ridden freight trains and hitchhiked all over the country. He'd written thousands of songs and played at hundreds of concerts to support working people who were striking for a living wage and people who were struggling to stop wars and bring peace to the United States.

Pete had always cared about the earth and his fellow humans, but in 1964 he was turned in a new direction. He read Rachel Carson's *Silent Spring*. Suddenly he realized that his country and the earth and the broad, shining Hudson River were all in danger. The world was turning into a garbage dump! That's when Pete organized fund-raising picnics all through the Hudson River valley, and with the money, he and his friends built the tall, elegant *Clearwater*. Everywhere the sailboat went, it brought the message, "Save the river!"

The *Clearwater* still sails the river. And each year there's a Clearwater Festival on shore with music, dancing, and storytelling. There's good food, fun, and—besides the message "Save the river!"—the boat reminds people to "Save the world!" The waters are cleaner now. New York State and the federal government have passed environmental laws like the Clean Water Act to stop polluters. But there's still plenty to fight for. Very harmful chemicals called PCBs, which factories spilled into the Hudson years ago, are still there and need to be fully and safely removed. And builders are allowed to crowd the wooded banks of the Hudson with high-rise buildings that shut the rest of us off from the great river. Pete Seeger's struggle goes on.

> *Gotta lift your heart*
> *Out on this broad, old river*
> *Y'gotta understand*
> *We got a job to do.*
> *If we work together*
> *In all kinds of weather*
> *Before you know it this mighty river*
> *Will run clear through.*

—from "Broad Old River"
music and words by Pete Seeger

Chico Mendes

(b. 1944 – d. 1988)

When Chico looked up from the floor of the Brazilian rain forest, he couldn't see the sky. Layers and layers of leaves, shrubs, vines, small trees, and finally, great, giant trees blocked the sun. Rain trickled slowly down from layer to layer, through the twilight, plopped onto Chico's nose, and then dropped to the mossy earth. Chico loved the trilling and squawking of millions of brightly colored birds and the whispering flit of tree frogs and insects.

He started working in the forest with his father when he was nine. They were rubber tappers. They went from rubber tree to rubber tree, cutting thin slits in the bark and collecting the milky white fluid that came out. Factories turned the fluid into latex that was used for tires, pencil erasers, athletic shoes, and other products. "The rubber tree is like our mother," Chico's cousin explained. "Her milk is like our blood. Each year she gives us so much."

By the time Chico had grown into a chunky man with crinkly, smiling eyes, a thick mustache, and curly black hair, the rain forest was beginning to change. The government of Brazil built a road through the forest and sent in settlers, ranchers, and loggers. They began to cut down the huge, ancient trees for lumber and burn the brush and smaller trees to clear land for farming. Black smoke, the whine of chain saws, and the crackle and crash of falling trees were everywhere. Each year large sections—if added together, as big as the state of Washington—were being wiped out.

Chico joined a national workers' union and led his fellow rubber tappers in a fight to save the forest. They rushed through the shadowy woods to the dry, sunny cutting areas. They argued with the workers or linked arms in human chains to protect the big trees. He even made a trip to Washington, D. C., to beg the U. S. Congress to urge Brazil to save the rain forest. The United Nations gave him an award for his work,

and environmentalists began to pay attention to the destruction. But the cutting continued.

Cattle ranchers, farmers, and loggers began striking back at people who wanted to save the rain forest. Rubber tappers, who were friends of Chico, were attacked. Their houses were burned to the ground, and some of them were even murdered. Chico Mendes was warned to get out and to stop his fight, otherwise he'd be killed too. But he had a wife and two children by this time. He answered, "I have to save the trees for our children. I can't run away."

One night in 1988 Chico Mendes was shot to death in the backyard of his home. Two cattle ranchers went to prison for the crime. The destruction of rain forests in Brazil, Indonesia, and other parts of the world goes on. Conservation organizations are trying to stop it, or at least to slow it down. Chico did his best. The groups are trying to continue his work.

DID YOU KNOW?

Children who live in villages of the Amazon, like children in many places, love to keep pets. But there's no shopping mall and no pet store with kittens and puppies. In most cases, kids here get a pet when their father goes into the forest to hunt or to chop down a tree. He comes across a wild animal, such as a snake or a bird, and takes the animal home to his kids. It's then raised as best the human family knows how. But without a vet nearby, most animals brought in from the wild don't live long. This little girl is obviously very fond of her woolly monkey. (Photo by Roger Harris. Courtesy of junglephotos.com)

DANGEROUS PROTESTS

Chico Mendes protested and risked his life for the rain forest—and lost. Other environmentalists have chained themselves to trees (for a while) to discourage their destruction. But nine members of the group Earth First!—who were concerned about the lumber industry's extensive removal of trees in Northern California—took their protest to a very great height. Waving their "Save the Trees" banners, they climbed the cables of the Golden Gate Bridge in San Francisco. They caused a six-hour traffic jam on the bridge and ended up in jail. It's much safer to write letters to Congress—and that way you won't scare your family!

Jane Goodall

(b. 1934 –)

DID YOU KNOW?

Jane Goodall started an organization called Roots & Shoots for young people from kindergarten to college age. There are branches all over the world, where kids do ecology projects together, help out at animal shelters and zoos, and learn about the environment. Look up "Roots & Shoots" on the Internet for more information.

Jane loved animals so much that as a toddler she took a pile of garden worms to bed with her. Luckily her mother discovered the squiggly worms before they got squashed. She explained that worms would die in bed—they needed to be in the earth. And Jane rushed them back out to the garden.

As an adult, Jane's love of animals carried her from her home in England all the way to Africa, where she worked with a famous anthropologist, Dr. Louis Leakey. The animals they found weren't cuddly. They were the fossilized bones of animals hundreds of thousands of years old. As Dr. Leakey and Jane dug into the side of a deep gorge, they also found many simple stone tools made by ancient humans. And finally they dug up the skull of a human male with such strong jaws and large teeth that they called him "nutcracker man." How did these earliest humans live, eat, and mate, wondered Dr. Leakey. We might understand them better, he thought, if we studied our closest relatives, the chimpanzees.

"I'll do it!" said Jane. "I'll study them. "That decision changed the rest of her life.

With Louis Leakey's help, Jane set up a camp in the forest beside a huge lake in Tanzania, Africa. She began to walk through the forest and climb the mountains. At first she caught only glimpses of the chimps as they swung through the tall trees and ate fruit high in the treetops. Sometimes she knew the chimps were nearby when fruit peels started dropping on her head. It took almost a year of following them silently before the chimps began to accept this blonde, pony-tailed "white ape." And for the next 40 years, and hopefully for many more to come, Jane has been following and studying the chimps as they eat, nurse their babies, hug and groom each other, wrestle, and squabble.

Jane gives each chimp a name. Some of them have become her friends. There was David Graybeard—who reached out to touch her one day—Flo, Goblin, and others.

Wilkie gazes out from a tree in Gombe National Park, Tanzania, Africa. In the early 1990s, Wilkie was the "alpha male" of his group, until he was challenged by the next leader, a chimp named Freud. (Courtesy of The Jane Goodall Institute)

And they seemed so human. They used twigs and leaves as tools to get at ants and honey. They kissed and tickled each other. Jane thought they were kinder and gentler than humans until, after a while, she saw females attacking the babies of other females, and males ganging up to take over land from other groups of chimps. Sadly, she realized that chimps, like humans, are not always kind to one another.

When Jane left the forest to attend conferences or make speeches about her work, she found that the world outside was changing. Cities were growing, waste was being dumped or pumped into fields, oceans, and lakes, and wild animals and birds were dying. Jane threw herself into the battle to save the wild places and wild animals of the earth. Today, in her 70s (her ponytail is white now), she travels the world fighting to convince all of us to protect the environment. And she warns those of us who live in the rich countries of the world to stop our wasteful use of natural resources.

Jane Goodall's message is clear—Don't shrug your shoulders and say, "What difference would *I* make?" Each one of us matters. If each of us shows respect and responsibility for our Earth, we'll save it! But hurry—time is running out!

When she's tired of lecturing, Jane comes back to the quiet of her lakeside camp, to the great trees and to her friends the chimps. The peace and beauty of sunrises, sunsets, and birdsongs fill her again and keep her strong enough to keep fighting.

DID YOU KNOW?

Chimpanzees are "knuckle-walkers." They walk on all fours and use their knuckles for support. They can extend their arms, which are longer than their legs, to reach fruits on branches too light to support the weight of a chimp. And, of course, those arms are also perfect for swinging through the trees.

Yossi Leshem

(b. 1947 –)

On holiday mornings Yossi's mother would call, "Put away your toys, Yossi. We're going hiking." He'd jump up, eager to get going. Yossi's parents had come to Israel from Germany, where hiking is a national sport, and their home in Haifa was near the Carmel Forest, full of trails and nature to explore.

It wasn't so much nature or animals that interested Yossi's parents. He said years later about his mother that she couldn't tell the difference between a fox and a field mouse—she just loved walking. So did Yossi. But he soon learned a great deal about foxes, field mice, and other wild things, and became a leader of the Society for the Preservation of Nature in Israel.

Most interesting of all to him were the huge, swirling flocks of birds that swept over the Carmel Forest and the Jordan Valley as they migrated to new homes in the spring and fall of each year. Five hundred million birds migrate through Israel's skies twice a year. To Yossi they seemed powerful and free, riding the wind over lakes and forests and national borders. But they were dangerous, too. The great flocks sometimes burst out of the clouds and accidentally crashed into Israeli aircraft. Over the years hundreds of birds were killed, and many planes were damaged. Some even crashed.

As a university student working to earn a doctoral degree, Yossi tackled the problem of deadly collisions between birds and planes. He and his fellow researcher, Ehud Dovrat, convinced Tel Aviv University, the Israeli Air Force, and the Israeli Ministry of Science to work

with them in a study. They would do this study while flying along-side the migrating flocks of birds.

Yossi and Ehud found a motorized glider that could coast quietly, keeping pace with the birds without frightening them. The glider flew up, searching for birds. When the pilot found a flock, he shut off the engine and soared and glided silently, wing to wing with the birds. As the pilots flew, they learned the routes that various species of birds like to take, the altitudes at which they fly, the times in the spring and fall that they migrate, and much more. From the ground, radar stations tracked the flocks. And some of the birds were fitted with tiny radio transmitters that "beeped" their positions. The poor birds—their privacy was gone. But they were saved from fatal air-traffic

With its motor turned off this glider flew silently beside great flocks of migrating birds and reported their positions to watchers on the ground. (Photo by Yossi Leshem)

accidents because planes could now be warned away from their routes. As a result of the work by Yossi and Ehud, collisions between birds and planes dropped by 88 percent!

Bird tracking for Yossi has become even more exciting as other countries have begun taking part. Israeli and German scientists, working together, decided to attach transmitters to the backs of white storks. The birds' migration was then tracked by satellites high in the sky across a series of national borders. (In case you're worried—the transmitters are lightweight and don't affect the bird's flight.) On an Israeli government Web site in 1994–95, children were able to follow the special travels of a stork named Princess and her mate Jonah.

As the story unfolded on the Internet, on a Web page called "Migrating Birds Know No Boundaries," both storks left France in the fall—on separate vacations. Jonah flew to Spain for the winter, and Princess made her way south to faraway Cape Town, South Africa. In the spring, Princess returned to France and found Jonah already at home, preparing their nest for a new batch of eggs!

So, we've learned that migrating birds know no boundaries. Yossi hopes that Israel and its neighboring countries may learn from the birds—how to cross national borders and work together. Groups in Jordan, the Palestinian Authority, and Israel are already sharing information. Russian kids have come to visit the International Center for the Study of Bird Migration in Latrun, Israel, and many other countries are interested.

What's next for Yossi Leshem? He's involved in a huge project of preserving birds' migration routes along the 22 countries of the Great Rift Valley (through Asia and Africa), and a barn-owl project for biological pest control, and more and more. Like the birds, Yossi Leshem knows no boundaries!

Great egrets roost in huge flocks along the Samiria River in the Pacaya-Samiria Reserve, west of Iquitos, Peru. (Photo by Roger Harris. Courtesy of junglephotos.com)

WHO NEEDS A RAIN FOREST?

We do! But we have to think about the reasons. Just looking at it, the rain forest doesn't look too useful. No farmland, coal, or oil. Just trees, bugs, and birds. What purpose does a rain forest serve, and what does one look like?

The best-known rain forest, called the Amazon, is the largest in the world. It's huge—bigger than all of Europe. Mile after mile of giant trees form a tight cover of green leaves. And underneath there are two or three more layers of smaller trees and bushes. All of this greenery sparkles with hundreds of species of birds of all colors, swooping and fluttering through the leafy twilight. Along with them live thousands of species of butterflies, beetles, and other insects. Monkeys swing through the trees; jaguars stalk beneath them. Deer, iguanas, turtles, and other creatures also live in the forest. Their nourishment comes from the ways in which they feed off each other and from the almost constant drip of rain all throughout the year. And all that moisture is carried by the winds to other places. So rain forests play a very important part in the rest of the world's weather.

Rain forests cover 7 percent of the earth's surface, and many of the plant and animal species of the earth live among their roots, leaves, and branches. Tribes of Indians live in the

Amazon rain forest, too. In chapter 8 we learned about the combinations of chemical substances that scientists have drawn from plants to use for medicines. Some of these were medications the Indians had discovered long before. The countless species of plants we haven't yet discovered could hold many more cures for us.

This very minute, the forest is working for the earth in even another way. It's a giant sponge, soaking up carbon dioxide, including the excess carbon dioxide created by car exhaust and factory processes. Then it breathes out life-giving oxygen. Rain forests and other forests work constantly against air pollution and global warming.

Some of the countries that contain rain forests don't know or care about their beauty or usefulness. They cut down the giant trees, sell them for lumber and then burn the smaller trees to clear the land for farming. But the thin soil will produce grass or food for only two or three years. It's not good crop-growing land—it's only good forest land.

The World Bank, which was organized by the United Nations to help needy countries, speeded up the destruction of the Brazilian rain forest by lending Brazil money to build a road through the great trees. Then busloads of farmers, loggers, and miners came streaming in to carve out camps and farms for themselves. Today the World Bank has changed its policy. When it lends money for land development, it demands that some of the land be set aside as forest preserves and that tribes of local Indians be protected. There may still be hope for one of our Earth's natural treasures.

The Amazon rain forest is home to more than 12 kinds of toucans. A toucan's bill is almost hollow, so it's very lightweight. The bill helps the toucan reach fruits at the end of long branches or probe into tree holes for other food, like bird eggs or small animals. Toucans live so high in the forest canopy that it's hard to see them. This photograph was taken in a Colombian zoo. (Photo by Roger Harris. Courtesy of junglephotos.com)

The spectacled caiman is the most common species in the Amazon rain forest. Its name comes from the bony ridges across its snout. As with all reptiles, caimans rely on the sun to heat their bodies. When it wants to cool down, a caiman can move into the shade of a tree or slither into the water. This one is basking beside a pond that is covered in "water lettuce." Look closely and you will see the caiman has a pal. (Photo by Roger Harris. Courtesy of junglephotos.com)

All the busy, day-and-night activity of ants, porcupines, bacteria, ibexes, hawks, and lizards is mostly invisible to these tourists visiting the desert in Jordan. Life is bustling under the sand and between the cliffs of this arid land. (Photo by Chaya M. Burstein)

WHO NEEDS A DESERT?

Israel does—and so does much of the rest of the world. Two-thirds of tiny Israel is desert, partly Judean desert in the center and mostly Negev desert in the south. And 4 percent of the rest of the world is desert, which means an area that gets less than 10 inches of rain a year. Central Africa, huge chunks of China, parts of the American southwest, much of the Middle East, and other areas are desert.

Desert isn't necessarily dead wasteland, good only for filming Wild West movies. With only

An ibex is a species of large wild goat. When ibexes travel to a water hole, one member of the group keeps watch and whistles if danger approaches, letting the herd know to race to the desert cliffs. With strong, agile legs and grooved hooves, they then climb the rocks to reach safety. (Courtesy of Israelimages.com)

10 inches of rain, Israel's northern Negev sparkles with wildflowers each spring. Further south, with even less rain, living creatures work day and night in the dry earth, keeping it

fruitful. Under the ground, termite ants busily gather and store seeds, leaves, and other bits of vegetable matter. The buried seeds sprout and make green food for the ibexes—wild goats that climb hillsides, churning up the hard-crusted soil, and leaving droppings for fertilizer. Prickly bushes make shady havens for seeds washed down by sudden rains. Desert porcupines dig pits as they hunt for food, and the pits gather dew, seeds, and energetic bacteria that make food for new, young plants.

Not only ants and porcupines live in the desert. People can live there, too, if they respect and care for it. Archaeologists have found the ruined cities of an ancient people called Nabateans, who lived in the desert of the Negev for a thousand years. They used the desert just as the termite ants and the ibexes did (and still do). They dug ditches to catch the scarce rain water and channel it to their farms. They were able to grow enough food in the desert to feed passing camel caravans. The Nabateans accepted the desert's difficult conditions, such as the small amount of rain and limited underground water. They used the resources as efficiently as possible and helped keep the desert healthy.

Fifteen hundred years ago, the Nabateans built a city called Petra deep in the desert. Camel caravans and other travelers stopped here to rest. Tourists today in Jordan are fascinated by exploring the rose-red, stone ruins of the Nabateans' temples and homes. (Photo by Chaya M. Burstein)

Deserts are delicate. They can die for many reasons. Sometimes climate change cuts off their water. More often it's because we humans mistreat the soil through overfarming, overgrazing, or redirecting the natural water to other areas. Natural vegetation dies and the earth gets blown or washed away, leaving only barren rock or sand. This process is called "desertification."

Large parts of China and Central Africa are suffering from desertification. Sometimes it spreads like a disease, as waves of dry sand are blown across nearby, still-fertile soil and smother the vegetation. Only through careful planning of where and how to plant trees and crops, diversion of rainwater to prevent rapid "runoff" (rainwater that carries soil to streams), purification of wastewater, and other methods—will we keep the living deserts healthy. It's a challenge!

Pigeon Creek Kids

Pigeon Creek, which runs behind the Jackson Elementary School in Everett, Washington, was a mess! It was clogged with empty soda cans, soggy boxes, torn shoes, worn tires, and other junk. But Mr. King, the fifth-grade teacher, remembered when Pigeon Creek had been clear, sparkling, and jumping with salmon. As a boy, he'd seen young Pacific salmon swimming down the creek into the ocean, and two-foot-long, adult salmon swimming upstream to spawn (make baby salmon). Who could believe that now—looking at the muddy creek water oozing through a culvert into the ocean.

The school principal believed it. "Let's adopt Pigeon Creek," said the principal. "We'll clean the banks and the water and stock it with fish." It's worth a try, thought the fifth-graders. Maybe we could revive the stream, and maybe the salmon will come back.

First they went out with rakes, shovels, and trash bags, and climbed up and down the banks of Pigeon Creek. They pulled out tons of garbage and old bed springs, branches, and parts

This pail is loaded with wiggling baby salmon, about to be carried to their new life in Pigeon Creek. Hanging over the top edge is a portable air pump, ensuring that the fish get enough oxygen while they're being transported. Once everyone gets to the stream, the teacher scoops out a fish for each child and places it into an individual plastic bag of cool water. (Photo by Marilyn Whitford)

Since Mr. King's class made its first trip down to clean up Pigeon Creek in the mid-1980s, school kids have continued with the annual salmon project. First-grader Kaleb has given his fish a name—Chatterbox—and is getting ready to slide it into the stream. Kaleb's fourth-grade "buddy" Miciah is standing by for encouragement. It's not always easy to say good-bye to your baby salmon. (Photo by Marilyn Whitford)

Baby salmon are called "fry." They will live and grow in the freshwater stream for about a year before swimming to the salty ocean. By then they will have shiny, silver coats (the males turn orange only at spawning time) and a new name—"smolts." Jerry, Mitchell, and Nicole know that only some of the salmon will make it back to Pigeon Creek. Will theirs be one of the them? (Photo by Marilyn Whitford)

DID YOU KNOW?

A salmon sleeps with its eyes open. With no eyelids, it has no choice! When a salmon is awake, it can see very well what is happening on both sides of itself—all at once. Because it has an eye on each side of its head, a salmon doesn't have to turn its head like you and I do. That's handy when looking for something to eat— or guarding against getting eaten.

Salmon always return to the stream where they were born to have their young. This one is a chinook (also called "king" salmon). It sometimes grows to more than 100 pounds and is by far the largest species. The other four kinds of Pacific salmon are chum (or "dog"), coho ("silver"), pink ("humpy"), and sockeye ("red"). The salmon in Pigeon Creek are coho, which usually weigh no more than 12 pounds. (Courtesy of the U.S. Fish & Wildlife Service)

of cars that were clogging the water. Parents and city and county workers helped, too. And finally the stream burst forth and began to run clear. Then the kids stenciled signs next to the city's storm drains leading to the creek saying, "Dump No Waste—Drains to Stream."

Next, in mid-winter, the school bought a large fish tank, and the state hatchery gave the school a big batch of orange, pea-size salmon eggs. Over the next few weeks the students learned to keep the light dim around the tank, to keep the water temperature right, to check the oxygen level of the water, to clean the tank and—as soon as the little fish were ready—to sprinkle in the fish food.

Finally, in the spring, they carefully scooped out the wiggling, one-and-a-half-inch-long fish, put them in pails of water, and carried them out to Pigeon Creek, where—one by one— they let them go. The little fish would grow in the creek for as long as a year, and then they'd head out to the Pacific Ocean.

Would any come back? the kids wondered. Bigger fish or birds might eat them, or they'd get caught in the nets of fishing boats, or they'd get sick. A million bad things could happen to salmon in the huge ocean. So the Everett kids worried and waited. That winter and the next they cared for new batches of salmon eggs, but they kept waiting for their first salmon to come home.

One day, almost two years after the Jackson school kids had started hatching their first salmon eggs, a large, bright-orange salmon came swimming up the creek. It was coming home to spawn. And then a few more fish came, and a few more. After all this time and the kids' work and patience, some of the Pigeon Creek salmon had made it back! The kids were proud. Ecstatic! They'd made it happen. "Let's do it again and again," they said. And that's exactly what they're doing.

WE CAN DO IT!

CHICO, RACHEL, JANE, AARON, YOSSI AND PETE CAME FROM DIFFERENT PLACES AND HAD DIFFERENT BELIEFS. BUT THEY ALL AGREED ON ONE IMPORTANT THING. THEY HAD TO FIGHT IN THE BATTLE TO SAVE OUR EARTH AND ITS CREATURES.

BUT I THOUGHT THIS BOOK WAS ABOUT JEWISH ECOLOGY, ABOUT HOW JEWISH CUSTOMS ARE GOOD FOR THE EARTH.

EARTH

FOR SURE IT'S ABOUT JEWISH CUSTOMS, BUT IT'S ALSO ABOUT EVERYONE'S CUSTOMS AND ATTITUDES. BECAUSE WE'RE ALL IN THIS ROWBOAT TOGETHER — JEWS, MUSLIMS, CHRISTIANS, TREE WORSHIPPERS...

HOW ABOUT THE BIBLE'S 'TILL IT AND TEND IT.' DOES THAT STILL MAKE SENSE AFTER ALL THESE YEARS?

I NEED ONE MORE CHAPTER TO ANSWER THAT QUESTION.

LET'S GO!

11 Till It and Tend It, and More

Abraham, Sarah, and our other ancestors had a simple, natural connection to their flocks of sheep and goats, to the wild animals that raided their flocks, to the waterholes and rocks, and to the fields of wild berries and grains. The Bible and the Talmud say things like "don't destroy fruit trees" (*bal tash'hit*) and "have compassion for animals" (*tzaar baalei chaim*) and "leave open land (called a *migrash*) around each Levite city." These laws had clear meanings and helped people to understand how they should use their natural environment. The world belonged to God. People could use the good resources, but they shouldn't waste them. They shouldn't destroy plants and animals, except for essential, reasonable human needs.

Lumbermen are chopping down trees in Austria carefully, not "clear-cutting" the forest, but cutting selectively here and there. It's a compromise with *bal tash'hit*. (Photo by Chaya M. Burstein)

Centuries later the world's population suddenly exploded! Humans began to use bigger and bigger chunks of the world's resources. So then how helpful could those old laws be?

The old laws had to grow broader and be adjusted to meet the new conditions affecting animals and the earth.

Bal tash'hit, don't destroy, taught the Jews to respect fruit trees, even in wartime. Over the centuries the concept grew to mean protecting wild animals and forests. It warned against diverting water for our own use if doing so would then dry out our neighbors' lands. Today it's used to argue against chopping down forests, not because they're fruit trees, but because all trees help to keep our air breathable. And it makes the case against destroying the great variety of natural life we need and enjoy—the biodiversity of our planet.

Tzaar baalei chaim, compassion for animals, has made us think carefully about using animals for scientific experiments and about using cruel methods to raise and slaughter animals for food. And we even worry about the careless, sometimes brutal, use of animals for entertainment, as in circuses and rodeos.

Leaving a *migrash*—open land—around Levite cities was required by the Bible. Because the tribe of Levi didn't receive land, as did all the other tribes of Israel, it was given cities all through the country, as well as open land around the cities. The Bible's requirement can be a guide to modern city planners and to those who fight to save land for national parks and preserves.

Our earliest laws, the Ten Commandments, provide advice as well. The Fifth Commandment tells us to rest on the Sabbath and to have our families, guests, servants, and work animals also rest. The Sabbath, a day for relaxing, praying, and feeling the wonderfulness of God and the earth, is more important than making money and using the earth and its animals for gain. The Tenth Commandment tells us not to covet, which means not to

DID YOU KNOW?

The United States cuts down more trees each year than any other country in the world. But at least lumber companies are now required to plant young trees in areas where they cut down "old growth." In general, an old-growth forest is one that exists without human intrusions, much as it would have been in the days before European colonization. Today, these forests are often considered to be endangered habitats.

Cities need open space, the Bible tells us. What would the Levites (see chapter 4) think of Central Park in New York City? Maybe they would get out their ice skates. For certain, they would be impressed by the trees. The park's greenery reduces heat, filters out pollution, and acts as a noise buffer. Trees help keep the soil in place and their beauty softens the look and feel of the urban landscape (Photo by Sara Cedar Miller. Courtesy of the Central Park Conservancy)

be envious of other people for the things they have. Think about how that might affect decisions in your life or mine. How do we feel when we see someone getting the latest model television, throwing a spectacular party, wearing very costly clothing, or riding in a big new car? If we think that our families must do the same or better, is that coveting? Sometimes it is. And such constant need for more of everything can use up great amounts of the earth's limited resources.

Once we thought of our laws as applying only to the Promised Land and serving the God of Israel. Now we've learned that they apply to the whole world and that all living things are connected to each other and dependent on each other. So instead of interfering so much with animals and the earth, using up so many resources, and putting ourselves so often in the center of everything, we need to live in harmony with our natural community.

Sometimes our future on the earth seems scary. Even a sunny, upbeat writer like Jane Goodall compared the growing problems of our Earth with the movement of a great ship on the ocean. The pilot may see rocks close ahead and try desperately to turn the ship away. But the heavy ship can only turn slowly, and despite all efforts, it will be swept ahead by the water and crash into the rocks. It's a grim warning, but Goodall doesn't leave us shipwrecked. She ends up by saying that each of us can and must make changes to prevent the collision.

We can't say that only the government should take care of this, or the scientists, or the United Nations, or "big business," or the mayor, or our parents. They *all* should, and so should each of us. We can bring home a homeless kitten, plant a vegetable garden, eat the eggs of free-range chickens, or do many other things to show our love and gratitude for the beautiful, generous earth we live on. It's a rare haven in this strange solar system.

So have fun and enjoy the earth. Hike through the parks and forests, paddle down the rivers, have cookouts, swim in the oceans and play on the sand, read a book on a sunny bench, and dig in the garden. And when work has to be done to help the environment, remember the Talmud's advice— No one is expected to complete the whole job, but each person must do all that he or she can.

12 Mini-encyclopedia

A

Abraham   The father of the Jewish people. Abraham lived almost 4,000 years ago. According to the Bible, he was the first person to believe that there is but one God.

Acid rain   Contaminated air, full of chemical gases given off by factories and motor vehicles, which gets blown by the wind and washed into the earth by rain, fog, and snow. Acid rain pollutes lakes and streams, damages vegetation, and speeds up the decay of buildings and outdoor sculptures.

Adam and Eve   The first human beings, according to the Bible. The Book of Genesis tells how Adam and Eve lived in the Garden of Eden until they disobeyed God's rules and were driven out.

Afikoman   A symbolic piece of matzah that the leader of the Passover seder hides somewhere in the house. Toward the end of the seder, children hunt for the *afikoman*. They are rewarded for its return with money or a small toy. In some families, it's the children who hide the *afikoman*. Then they demand a prize for its safe return. Once recovered, the *afikoman* is divided and everyone gets a piece as "dessert," marking the end of the meal. Pronounced *ah-fee-KO-men*, it is a Hebrew word that comes from a Greek word that in fact means "dessert."

Africa   A huge continent south of Europe and west of Asia. Grasslands cover much of the land, and rain forests stand in western Africa near the equator. The largest desert in the world is in Africa (the Sahara), as well as the longest river (the Nile). Parts of Africa are home to a large, but shrinking, population of wild animals, such as elephants, chimpanzees, zebras, and lions. Most scientists believe the first human beings appeared in Africa. So many different kinds of people live there today that more than 1,000 languages can be heard.

Algae   Plants such as kelp and other seaweed that grow in lakes and waterways. If these plants get their nutrition from things washed into the water, like farm fertilizer, they grow excessively fast. Then the algae use up too much of the available oxygen and crowd out fish and other aquatic life.

Many of these terms appear in other places in the book. If you want to learn more, check the index.

Aravah Valley A deep cut in the earth's surface that runs along the border between Jordan and Israel, stretching south from the Dead Sea to the Gulf of Aqaba. It's a hot, dry area settled by a few Israeli communities that practice careful, water-conserving farming techniques.

Archaeologist A scientist who studies the objects and structures left by ancient, long-gone people and tries to understand their way of life.

Asteroids Rocky and metallic objects that orbit the sun but are too small to be considered planets. An asteroid that enters the earth's atmosphere is called a meteoroid. Traveling at high speed, it creates a streak of light known as a meteor. If the meteoroid does not burn up completely, the name changes to meteorite. Then it smashes into the earth's surface and makes a big depression referred to as a crater. Some scientists believe that the impact of a giant meteorite 65 million years ago raised enough flying rocks and dust to shut out the sun for centuries. This event may be what killed off much of the prehistoric vegetation and all of the dinosaurs.

Atmosphere An envelope of gases surrounding the earth. It is held in place by the pull of the earth's gravity. The atmosphere contains ozone, which protects life on our planet from the sun's harsh ultraviolet rays.

B

Babylonia An Asian empire of the sixth century B.C.E. centered in the area known as Iraq today. The Babylonians conquered the Jewish kingdom of Judea in 586 B.C.E., destroyed the Temple in Jerusalem, and exiled many Judeans.

Bal tash'hit Hebrew for "don't destroy." The Bible warns the Israelites, when they're at war, not to chop down the fruit trees that stand outside a besieged, walled city. This rule for protecting fruit trees has grown over the centuries to include caring for all trees and natural life.

B.C.E. An abbreviation used by Jews for marking dates that occurred "Before the Common Era." Many non-Jews use a different abbreviation called B.C.

Bible A text made up of the earliest teachings, history, and traditions of the Jewish people. The first five books of the Bible are the Torah. They are written in Hebrew on a continuous parchment scroll housed in the Holy Ark—a special cabinet in the synagogue. Members of the congregation read aloud from the Torah on the Sabbath and some of the holidays. The two other sections of the Bible are called Prophets and Writings.

Biodegradable items Materials or products that can be broken down by bacteria to become part of the natural environment again.

Biodiversity The huge number and variety of living things on the earth. Some scientists estimate that there are 7 to 10 million different species. Other scientists believe there may be as many as 100 million—most of them still undiscovered! All species (including we humans) affect and depend on each other in countless ways. For example, plants absorb carbon dioxide and release oxygen, keeping the earth's air breathable. Bacteria decompose plant and animal waste and remains, so that living things can feed the soil.

Biofuels Fuels made from renewable sources such as corn, soybeans, and leftover grease from restaurant food. Burgerfuel, anyone?

Biologist A scientist who studies plants, animals, and other living things to learn how they live, grow, and evolve.

Brazil The biggest country in South America. It contains most of the world's largest tropical rain forest—the Amazon.

Cain The older son of Adam and Eve. According to the Bible, he became the world's first murderer when he killed his brother, Abel.

Carbon dioxide A colorless, odorless gas that occurs naturally in the atmospheres of many planets, including that of the earth. All our green plants must absorb carbon dioxide to live and grow. They convert carbon

dioxide and water into food and oxygen. When organic materials are burned—in a forest fire, a manufacturing process, or a car's engine— carbon dioxide gets added to the atmosphere. Too much carbon dioxide can be a problem. In the past 100 years, carbon dioxide in the earth's atmosphere has increased 25 percent. This increase is one cause of global warming.

C.E. An abbreviation used by Jews for marking dates in the "Common Era." The Common Era is a time period that started more than two thousand years ago and continues today. Many non-Jews use a different abbreviation called A.D.

Challah A braided bread, rich with eggs, traditionally eaten on the Sabbath and almost every Jewish holiday. Challahs at Rosh Hashanah are made in a round shape to celebrate the fullness of the New Year and the circular nature of the calendar.

Compost Decomposed organic materials (things with plant or animal origins) such as grass clippings, leaves, and kitchen waste. People create compost mixtures as a natural fertilizer —to provide nutrients for the soil of gardens and farms. Compost can also serve as mulch to keep the soil moist and reduce the number of weeds.

D

David The second king of Israel, who lived 3,000 years ago. As a boy, he fought a Philistine named Goliath. Later he became a powerful military leader as well as a writer of eloquent poetry. Rabbis believe he may have been the writer of the Book of Psalms in the Bible.

DDT A once-popular pesticide. Scientists created it for a good reason—to prevent malaria, typhus, and other insect-borne diseases in humans. But DDT ended up poisoning more than just mosquitoes—most notably birds and fish. The United States and other developed nations banned DDT in the 1970s, but it is still used in many countries.

Desert An area of land that receives less than 10 inches of rain a year and therefore has very little vegetation. Approximately one-third of the earth's land surface is desert. A desert landscape can include sand dunes, as in Saudi Arabia, or the bare rock of the Middle Eastern Sinai and the southwestern United States.

Developed countries Nations that have developed both their technology and their sense of social responsibility to provide a good standard of living for their populations. Most people in these countries have food, education, health care, and decent housing.

Drip irrigation A system of watering plants by laying down a hose that has a hole in it for each plant. The water drips out slowly and evenly. Drip irrigation uses much less water than spraying an entire area with a sprinkler.

E

Earth The third planet from the sun in a solar system that contains at least eight other planets, their moons, and smaller bodies. As far as we know, Earth is the only planet in the solar system that supports life.

Eco-groups Organizations that fight to preserve and protect our natural environment. Some, such as the Nature Conservancy, buy wild areas to prevent them from being built on or paved over. Others, such as Greenpeace International, fight for laws to protect the environment. The Coalition on the Environment and Jewish Life (COEJL) works to deepen the link between Jewish traditions and our concern for the natural world.

Ecology   The study of how living things interact with each other and with the places they live. To work in the field of ecology, it's important to be curious about the earth and to enjoy life sciences, such as botany, zoology, and biology. It's also helpful to be strong in writing and public speaking, in order to communicate well with the public about protecting the environment.

Egypt   Israel's southwestern neighbor. During a famine, the ancient Hebrews left Israel to live in Egypt, but they became enslaved there. Years later, they escaped and eventually made their way through the Sinai desert and back to Israel. At the Passover holiday, Jews celebrate this escape from slavery.

Energy   A force or power that makes things happen. There are many forms of energy. They range from the hardworking, sweaty energy of individual human beings to the nuclear energy produced by splitting the nucleus of an atom.

Environment   The area and life that surround a living thing. Your own environment may be a city, farm, suburb, desert, mountain, seaside, or forest. Each plant and animal is affected *by* its environment and has an effect *on* its environment. As the environmentalist John Muir said, "When we tug at a single thing in nature, we find it attached to the rest of the world."

Environmental Protection Agency (EPA)   An agency of the United States government. It oversees controls to make the air and water cleaner, and it monitors environmental problems that could affect our health. The EPA also takes steps to repair or clean up areas

that have suffered from environmental damage such as oil spills. Some of the people who work for the EPA devote their time to educating Americans about ways to protect and improve the environment.

European Union   An organization of countries whose member nations have opened their borders to each other and are trying to maintain a joint economic policy. It's known as "free trade." Most EU members now use a common currency called the euro, instead of each country having its own kind of money. The EU is establishing policies to help protect the environment by controlling pollution and waste disposal and by recycling used materials.

Evolution   A gradual process in which a living organism changes into a different, usually more complicated, form. People still argue about whether human beings appeared on Earth looking exactly like they do today, or whether they evolved from other, simpler forms over millions or even billions of years.

Exhaust   The fumes that are produced by burning fuel in an engine. Exhaust contains carbon dioxide and other gases that contribute to global warming.

Extinct species   A class of plants or animals that has died out. Some entire groups, such as the dinosaurs, disappeared long ago because of natural changes in the environment. But many species are becoming extinct because humans are killing them directly or destroying their habitats. Scientists estimate that we lose 30,000 species each year.

F

Fertilizer   Food for plants, which can come from organic materials such as compost or manure or from chemical compounds such as potash.

Fossil fuels   Energy sources made of fossils that were once living vegetation or marine microorganisms. Coal is fossilized wood, and oil and natural gas are fossilized plants. They changed into these forms after being compressed for millions of years. When fossil fuels burn, they release carbon dioxide.

Free-range animals   Farm animals that are allowed to range and forage with relative freedom. Chickens peck the earth for worms instead of being closed up all the time in chicken houses. Cattle roam around and graze on grass rather than living confined to feed lots. Famers who raise free-range animals are providing us with what may be the most

healthful eggs and meat. And they are meeting the Jewish directive of *tzaar baalei chaim*, caring about living creatures.

Fumigant   A vapor or gas used to kill animal pests such as rodents and insects in farm fields.

Fungus   A plantlike organism that has no chlorophyll, so it does not make its own food. A fungus draws its food from other living things. Molds and mushrooms are funguses.

G

Garden of Eden   A green, fruit-filled land with rivers running through it, which the Bible describes as the first home for all the earth's creatures.

Genes   Bits of information, contained in the cells of living things, which are inherited from earlier generations. They determine the many characteristics of the organism. For instance, because of your particular genes, you may have blue eyes like your grandmother and wavy hair like your grandfather.

Genesis   The first book in the Bible. It tells about many things, such as God's creation of the heavens, the earth, and all the plants and animals. Genesis also relates how Noah's ark was built in expectation of the Flood, how God made Abraham the first leader of the Jewish people, and how Joseph's own brothers sold him into slavery. The Hebrew name for the book is *Bereshit* (buh-ray-SHEET), which means "In the beginning."

Genetic modification
Changing the nature of a cell by removing a gene from it or by introducing other genes that change the original gene. Scientists do this for many reasons. One is to eliminate insect pests on farm crops, another is to make tomatoes that stay firm longer, and yet another is to cure human illnesses. Genetic modification is controversial, which means people do not always agree on whether or not it is a good idea.

Geothermal power
Electricity generated by using naturally occurring steam from geysers or hot springs and other deep-earth sources. It's a form of renewable energy.

Glaciers   Huge fields of ice and compacted snow that flow (advance and retreat) in response to changes in climate. Glaciers are found mostly at the North and South Poles, but every continent in the world (even Africa) has glaciers.

They once covered much of North America and Europe during the last Ice Age.

Global warming   A slow increase in the earth's average temperature, thought to be caused by an excess of greenhouse gases. This increase can produce harmful changes in wind patterns and the climate. Many scientists are worried about global warming because they believe it is causing the earth's glaciers to melt too fast. With a lot of melting, the levels of the oceans could eventually rise and cause severe flooding.

Great Britain   A Western European country that was given control of Palestine by the League of Nations after the First World War. This action was meant to establish a Jewish home-land within the borders of Palestine.

Green architecture   A type of design for buildings that takes the environment into consideration. The building is positioned to be warmed by the sun and cooled by breezes. It might have cisterns for collecting rainwater and skylights for natural lighting. If possible, recycled materials will be used for construction. The furnishings and carpeting inside will be made of materials that do not make people feel sick or cause allergies.

Greenhouse effect An atmospheric process that keeps the earth at a livable, pleasant temperature. Scientists named this process the greenhouse effect because it resembles the way a greenhouse keeps plants warm. When human activity intensifies the effect by putting more and more gases—such as methane and carbon dioxide—into the atmosphere, too much heat gets trapped. The result can be a potentially dangerous, overall rise in the earth's temperature.

H

Hadrian A Roman emperor who ruled over Judea (a kingdom in ancient Israel) in the second century C.E. He crushed the last, major Jewish rebellion against Rome, which was led by a warrior called Bar Kochba.

Ha-gomel A Hebrew prayer of thanks that Jews recite in a public setting, typically a synagogue, after certain events—escaping great danger, completing a long and difficult trip, or recovering from a serious illness or accident. *Ha-gomel* (hah-go-MELL) is loosely translated to mean "who bestows benefits."

Haifa A port city in northern Israel. It is built along the shore of the Mediterranean Sea and up the steep hillsides of Mount Carmel.

Hasidism *See Israel Ben Eliezer*

Hillel A great teacher, rabbi, and important contributor to the Talmud. He lived from about 60 to 9 B.C.E. Hillel's teachings always showed his gentleness and understanding. His best known instruction is: "Do not do to others what you would not want done to yourself. This is the whole law; the rest is commentary. Go and study."

Human A member of the animal species *Homo sapiens*, which is Latin for "wise human." Scientists believe that the first humans developed in central Africa and began to spread to other areas about 100,000 years ago.

Hybrid vehicles
Transportation powered by more than one energy source, thereby using fuel more efficiently. Hybrid cars typically use gasoline and then switch to electric power stored in batteries. Submarines are hybrids— either nuclear-electric or diesel-electric. Even a moped (motorized pedal bike) is a type of hybrid because it combines the power of a gasoline engine with the pedal power of its rider.

Hydraulic power Water power captured from water-falls, spillage from dams, and the movement of surf and tides. It can be used directly to move mechanical equipment, such as a water wheel, or stored to generate electricity (called hydro-electric or hydropower).

I

Incinerator A furnace that disposes of trash by burning it to ashes. Screens on the incinerator's smokestack can keep particles of burning trash from flying out, but polluting gases can still escape into the air.

Industrial revolution The period of invention and widespread use of power-driven equipment to speed up manufacturing. The revolution blossomed in the 18th century with the development of steam and water power. Then it grew even faster and bigger with the coming of electricity and inexpensive steel. Farmers were able to produce more food, and factories could make more goods. Cities expanded, population increased, and so did environmental pollution.

Intergalactic vehicles
Spaceships that travel between galaxies (large groups of stars). Today these ships only exist in science fiction but, for sure, they're coming!

International Center for the Study of Bird Migration
A research and education center founded by the Society for the Protection of Nature in Israel and by Tel Aviv University. Scientists from many countries work together planning studies about migrating birds and recording information as the birds fly across continents.

Isaiah A Hebrew prophet who scolded the rich and powerful leaders of Judea for their cruel, extravagant behavior and warned them that enemy countries would attack Judea as God's punishment. But he also predicted that eventually there would be a glowing peace and happiness for the Jewish people and for all the peoples of the world. Isaiah lived during the eighth and seventh centuries B.C.E., and his teachings are part of the Prophets section of the Bible.

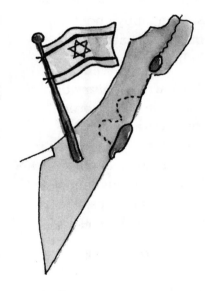

Israel A small country (about the size of New Jersey) at the southwestern corner of the continent of Asia. According to the Book of Genesis in the Bible, it was promised to the Jewish people as a homeland. The kingdom of Judea, part of biblical Israel, was destroyed by the Roman Empire in 70 C.E. But in 1948, after almost 2,000 years of exile from their land, the Jewish people established the modern State of Israel.

Israel Ben Eliezer A great spiritual leader in Russia in the 1700s. Israel Ben Eliezer became known as the Baal Shem Tov, the "master of a good name," and the founder of the Jewish religious movement Hasidism. He taught his followers that closeness to God could be expressed through joyous prayer, singing, and dancing, rather than solely by spending long hours of study in synagogues and study halls. His teachings gave even poor and uneducated people an honorable place in the community's religious life.

J

Jeremiah A Hebrew prophet of the seventh and sixth centuries B.C.E. He protested against the idol worship and the social injustice in Judea, and he warned that the kingdom would fall. Jeremiah would live to see the Babylonians destroy the First Temple. According to tradition, he sadly wrote the Book of Lamentations, found in the second section of the Bible, which describes the despair and desolation of Judea after the Babylonian conquest.

Jericho A town built around an oasis in the Jordan River valley. Based on studies of ancient ruins, archaeologists believe that Jericho is the oldest continuously lived-in settlement in the world.

Jerusalem The capital city of the modern State of Israel and the historic capital of the Israelite kingdom. The First and Second Temples were built here, and they were the destination of Jewish pilgrims from all over the world. Later, Jerusalem became a holy place for Christians and Muslims, too. The city has been captured and recaptured many times. Today Muslims and Jews are again disputing control of Jerusalem.

Jewish agricultural holidays Passover, Shavuot, Sukkot, as well as the days of counting the Omer. They are all based on the seasons of planting and harvesting in the ancient Land of Israel. In later centuries, when most Jews were no longer farmers, the holidays were given historical meanings that helped people remember and celebrate their history.

Jewish National Fund An organization that plants trees, drains swamps, and improves land for settlements in Israel. The fund was established in 1901 by the World Zionist Organization, which collected money from world Jewry to buy land in Palestine. This land became the property of the whole Jewish people and was used to establish settlements throughout the country.

Job A book of the Bible that tells the story of Job, a prosperous, happy, God-fearing man who suddenly suffers terrible misfortunes. "Why me?" he protests to God. "I've always been so good!" From out of a storm, God replies that only God knows all things, and human beings don't have the wisdom to question God's actions.

Jonah A reluctant prophet, whose story is told in the Bible. Jonah tried to escape God's command to save the city of Nineveh. In the end, following some time in the belly of a big fish, he decided he would travel to Nineveh after all. He was still unhappy about going, but he was able to succeed in his mission.

Jordan A country on the east side of the Jordan River (Israel's eastern boundary), established in 1946. Its official name is the Hashemite Kingdom of Jordan—and, yes, it is indeed ruled by a king.

Jordan River One of the most famous rivers in the world because it's mentioned many times in the Bible and other literature. The Jordan is the only real river in Israel, because the other waterways are smaller and usually have water only during the rainy season. The Jordan is fed from the north and east by mountain streams in Lebanon, Syria, and Jordan. The river flows south until it empties into the Dead Sea.

K

Kaddish   A prayer in praise of God. It has different forms—one is a mourner's prayer recited at the graves of family members and at memorial times, such as during the Yom Kippur service. This prayer actually makes no mention of death. The language of *Kaddish* is not Hebrew, but Aramaic, which was the everyday language spoken by Jews of long ago. It is written using the Hebrew alphabet.

Kosher   Hebrew for "fit" or "suitable." Most often the word is used to describe food that is suitable for an observant Jew to eat. Standards for the kinds of food that are considered to be kosher are listed in the Bible and in later books of Jewish law. The slaughter of animals must be done in a certain way by a specially trained religious Jew, to avoid inflicting pain on the animal.

Kyoto Protocol   A legally binding international agreement to reduce emission of greenhouse gases that can cause climate change. This agreement was initially negotiated at a 1997 meeting held in Kyoto, Japan, and has been slowly making the rounds of world capitals for signatures. The Kyoto Protocol will only be effective if and when all the major industrialized nations sign it and then take action on promises to slow global warming. It is just one example of the many international conferences and agreements on the environment.

L

Legislation for the environment   Laws passed by the U.S. Congress and by state legislatures, such as the Endangered Species Act. That law protects the habitats of fish, wildlife, and plants that are listed as threatened or endangered. (Many of the species are known only to biologists, but they are nonetheless extremely important.) The Clean Water Act controls the dumping of pollutants into the country's waterways. Perhaps as we understand better the importance of issues such as biological diversity, we'll pass additional legislation to protect our natural environment.

Levites   Members or descendants of the tribe of Levi. Moses, his brother Aaron, and his sister Miriam were Levites. During the 40-year trek through the desert, the Levites carried the Ark of the Covenant— the sacred container holding the tablets on which the Ten Commandments were written. Later, in the days of the Temple in Jerusalem, the Levites assisted the High Priests (the *Kohanim*), and they sang in the choir.

Leviticus   The third book of the Five Books of Moses. It includes laws concerning Temple sacrifices in ancient days, the dietary laws for keeping kosher, as well as the famous advice to "love your neighbor as yourself." The Hebrew name for Leviticus is *Vayikra* (vah-YEEK-rah), which means "He called."

M

Mass transportation
Trains, buses, subways, streetcars, and monorails—each carrying a very large number of people. Mass transportation does much less damage to the environment than individual transportation such as automobiles. Cars use a lot of fossil fuel, but each one carries a small number of people—often only one. Mass transportation, even if it uses fossil fuel rather than electricity, can carry far more people per gallon of gasoline or diesel than a car can. And there are other benefits. Mass transportation means that less land gets carved up for multi-lane highways. And there can be fewer parking lots,

which have surfaces that will not let rain penetrate the earth beneath them.

Medicines from plants
Naturally grown cures for diseases. The rosy periwinkle plant from Madagascar provides a powerful drug that can cure many cases of leukemia. The aspirin that people take for a headache or a fever was originally made from the leaves of a willow tree. These drugs are just two of the hundreds of medicines that we extract from plants and funguses. If we help the earth maintain a great variety of natural life, we may help ourselves find a great variety of medicinal cures.

FOX GLOVE

Mesopotamia
An ancient region of southwestern Asia, now in Iraq, between the Tigris and Euphrates rivers. (Its name comes from the Greek for "middle" and "river.") Mesopotamia is where the early civilizations of Akkad, Sumer, Babylonia, and Assyria were.

Messiah
One chosen by God to usher in a time of everlasting peace and justice for the Jewish people and the world. By Jewish tradition, the Messiah will be a descendant of King David. Various people throughout Jewish history declared themselves to be the Messiah, but the promised peace and justice did not appear.

Migration
Periodic movement from one region or climate to another for finding food or for breeding. In earlier history, humans migrated, wandering from place to place. Of course many varieties of animals continue to migrate. Among them are storks, penguins,

monarch butterflies, sea turtles, wood frogs, wilde-beests, and caribou. These migrations sometimes cause serious problems, as happens when birds migrate through air space that is crowded with jet traffic.

Moses   The prophet and great leader who brought the Jews out of slavery in Egypt about 3,500 years ago. He led them to Mount Sinai, where they received the Ten Commandments. Over the next 40 years, Moses guided his people and helped them become a nation, at which point they were ready to enter the Promised Land. The story of Moses is told in the Torah.

Moses Maimonides   A renowned Jewish philosopher, writer, and physician who lived in Egypt in the 12th and 13th centuries C.E. In his writings, he clarified and modernized the teachings of the Bible and the Talmud. Moses Maimonides was so highly respected that people said of him, "From Moses (in

the Bible) to Moses (Maimonides), there was none like Moses."

N

Native Americans or American Indians   The first humans to live in the Americas. They may have walked to the North American continent from Asia, at a time ages ago when the sea was low enough to expose a land bridge.

Negev   The Hebrew word for "south." The Negev desert includes almost the entire southern half of Israel. It is home to many Arab herdsmen and shepherds known as Bedouins. The Negev also contains Jewish

towns and settlements, some of which practice limited farming by using recycled water and water piped down from the north.

Network of protected lands   The 10 percent of the earth's land surface that has been set aside as preserves and national parks. Trees, plants, and animals can grow and reproduce in these places without the danger of exploitation by farmers, lumber companies, poachers, and miners. As the extinction of species continues, countries need to create more and larger areas of protected land to save our wild plants and animals.

Nineveh   An ancient city on the east bank of the

Tigris River. In Bible times, it was the capital city of Assyria. Its ruins are found in modern-day Iraq, near Mosul.

Noah   The man who was in charge of the ark during the biblical Flood. The Bible says that at God's command, the ark carried a pair of each of the earth's creatures. Noah's ark prevented the total extinction of life on Earth.

Nuclear energy   The heat released when the nucleus of an atom is split or fused. This heat is used for generating electric power. Nuclear energy (once called "atomic energy") seems like a cheap and unlimited source of power. Unfortunately, it produces dangerous radioactive waste, and that

waste remains a hazard for centuries. This is one of the reasons why individuals, environmental groups, and entire countries argue about whether or not nuclear energy is a good idea.

Omer   A 49-day period between the holidays of Passover and Shavuot when weddings and other celebrations are not held, except on the holiday of Lag ba-Omer. The Omer was once a tense time for Israeli farmers. It came during the season for planting and blossoming in the fields and orchards, and they were wary of drought. Through the centuries Jews have remembered the anxiety of this time, as well as certain sad events in Jewish history, and have avoided partying during the Omer. The Hebrew word *omer* (OH-mare) is often translated into English as "sheaf—a tied bundle of stalks." More precisely, *omer* means "a measure of dry things"—believed to be the

two quarts of barley flour presented to the Temple priests at Shavuot.

Organically grown fruits, vegetables, and grains
Food grown and processed without synthetic fertilizers or poisonous chemicals. Organic farmers feed their crop-yielding plants with natural fertilizers like manure and compost. They protect them from insects and rodents by various means—using pesticides derived from natural sources, bringing in natural predators such as owls, and sterilizing the pests so they cannot reproduce.

Overfishing   Harvesting such large numbers of fish from the oceans and rivers that various species of fish cannot reproduce quickly enough to survive. Huge, factory-like fishing ships carry sophisticated equipment to catch, clean, pack, and refrigerate the fish. This industrial method of fishing has emptied large sections of the world's oceans.

Oxygen   A gas that makes up 20 percent of the earth's atmosphere and is critical to our existence. Plants give off oxygen when using the sun's energy to make food. Animals need to take in oxygen when breathing. In addition, oxygen must be present for fire to take place. No oxygen, no toasted marshmallows.

Ozone layer   A protective layer in the earth's atmosphere that shields the planet's surface from the sun's harsh, ultraviolet radiation. Long-lasting chemicals such as fluorocarbons, once used in refrigerators and air conditioners, break down the ozone layer. This breakdown may, over time, harm people's skin and eyes and cause damage to farm crops.

Palestine   A name the Roman Empire gave to an area including the Land of Israel. Two thousand years later, after the First World War, Great Britain was charged with establishing a Jewish homeland in Palestine. After another 30 years, following a vote in the United Nations, the State of Israel declared its independence. Since then, there have been several bitter wars between Jews and Arabs. Some areas are now divided between the State of Israel and the Palestinian Authority, but the borders remain unclear.

Passover   One of the three pilgrimage holidays called for in the Bible. Jews would travel to the Temple in Jerusalem with gifts of first fruit and offerings to God. Then they would feast together. Today Passover is celebrated at a seder where the family eats a ceremonial meal and retells the story of the Israelites' escape from Egyptian slavery to freedom. The Hebrew name for Passover is Pesach (PAY-sakh).

Pesticides   Materials used to kill harmful insects, rodents, and funguses. These pests invade farmers' fields or come into our homes and backyards to dine on our food and plants. Some pesticides are made of chemicals that not only kill the pests, but also poison the soil, nearby waterways, and the natural predators that eat the pests. It's much better to use biological controls that interfere with the pests' life cycles.

Plastic   A man-made material used for everything from kids' toys to sewer pipes. Most plastic is not biodegradable, although it can usually be recycled. But if you do have to throw it away, be careful to dispose of it properly. For instance, sometimes fish and sea mammals suffocate when they try to swallow discarded plastic bags floating in the ocean.

Pollutant Any material that fouls or contaminates the soil, water, or air.

Population explosion A rapidly multiplying number of people being born and then also living longer. This situation can lead to people using up the resources of their own country, and those of the rest of the world, faster than the resources can be replaced. Ten thousand years ago, there were about five million human beings on the earth. Over the following 100 centuries, our population has grown to six billion. In modern times, this greatly expanded number of people has led to increased farming, lumbering, mining, and manufacturing. In turn, these have damaged the habitats and welfare of most other life on Earth.

Radar station A site where revolving "dishes" are mounted that can detect moving objects, even in the dark, even very far away. Radar is useful for airports, for ships at sea, for weather forecasting—and, of course, when searching for migrating flocks of birds, the way Yossi Leshem did in chapter 10. The word radar is short for "radio detection and ranging." That's because a transmitter at the station sends out pulses of high-frequency radio waves. These waves bounce off objects and return to the dish. A radar "echo" shows up on a monitor. A computer measures the time it takes for the signal to bounce off the targeted object and then

calculates how far away the object (or bird) is.

Radioactive waste The by-product of creating nuclear energy. Some medical equipment and some weapons of war also produce radioactive waste. Scientists have found no way to deactivate this dangerous material. We store it in lead-lined containers, bury the containers deep in the earth, and hope it doesn't leak out.

Rain forest A dense, ever-green forest with an average rainfall of about 100 inches a year. Rain forests can be tropical (very hot) as in the Amazon, or temperate (mild) as in the Pacific Northwest. In a rain forest, the huge number of trees are all taking in carbon dioxide to produce carbo-hydrates for their own growth (a process called photosynthesis). This removal of carbon dioxide helps to keep our air healthy.

Rashi A great rabbi, scholar, teacher, and winemaker who lived in France in the

11th and 12th centuries C.E. Rashi—the letters of his acronym come from **R**abbi **S**hlomo **B**en **Y**itzchak (Isaac)—wrote careful commentary and explanations of the Talmud, section by section. Later he also wrote a Bible commentary. His work still accompanies these books today.

Recycling   The process of reusing materials, sometimes in a changed form. Plastic bottles and aluminum cans can be melted down and turned into new bottles and cans. Rubber tires can be ground up and used as a soft surface under outdoor playground equipment. Recycling reduces the quantity of trash to be burned or buried, and it lessens our consumption of natural resources.

Renewable energy
Sources of energy that will not get used up. Sun, water, nuclear energy, and wind are sources we can use forever. Coal, natural gas and petroleum (oil) cannot rapidly renew themselves and will eventually run out.

Roman Empire   An ancient empire centered in Rome— the city that is now the capital of Italy. The Romans ruled much of Europe, North Africa, and Asia for more than a thousand years. Judea, a kingdom in the southern part of ancient Israel, fell under Roman control. Then in 70 C.E., after crushing the last of many Jewish rebellions, the Roman Empire captured Jerusalem and destroyed the Second Temple.

Rosh Hashanah   A holiday that falls on the first day of the Jewish calendar. Rosh Hashanah is a time when Jews think about how they have behaved during the previous year and about what changes they can make in themselves. They pray for a good year to come. The words Rosh Hashanah are Hebrew for "head of the year."

S

Sabbath   The seventh day of the week. The fifth of the Ten Commandments requires that each Jew and his or her family, servants, guests, and work animals must rest on the Sabbath. The Hebrew word for Sabbath is *Shabbat* (shah-BAHT). "*Shabbat* is a foretaste of Heaven," says a Jewish proverb.

Samson   The Israelite strong man whose story is told in the Bible. According to the Book of Judges, after being horribly treated by the Philistines who ruled over the Jews, Samson took revenge against them. He pulled down a building with the leaders inside, even though that meant he would die at the same time.

Sewage   Liquid and solid waste that is carried off by big pipes, usually underground. Sewage can be dumped on the soil and allowed to sink into the ground water. Or it can be sent flowing into streams, rivers, and oceans. Better yet, it can be taken to treatment plants and cleaned.

Shavuot   One of Judaism's three pilgrimage festivals, when the ancient Israelites traveled to the Temple in Jerusalem. Shavuot (Shah-VOO-ote) means "weeks" in Hebrew, and it is also known as the Harvest Festival and the Feast of Weeks. It marks the anniversary of Moses' receiving the Ten Commandments at Mount Sinai, and at the same time, it celebrates the first harvest of the fruits of spring.

Solar energy   A form of energy that is harnessed from the light of the sun's rays and used for purposes such as heating household and swimming-pool water and for general lighting, heating, and cooking. There are even studies underway to provide solar-powered cooling in the summer. Imagine the sun being used for air-conditioning!

Solar system   The name of the planetary system that contains our Earth. It's made up of the sun, the planets and their moons, along with asteroids,

comets, and other chunks of matter that orbit the sun. Scientists have discovered some other planetary systems that include sunlike stars, but none are anything like ours.

Solomon   The third king of ancient Israel. The son of King David, he was known for his wisdom, statesmanship, fairness, and poetry. The First Temple was built during King Solomon's reign.

Song of Songs   One of the five books referred to as a scroll or megillah, contained in Writings, the third section of the Bible. Thought to have been written by King Solomon, it is a series of love poems often described as representing the love between God and the Israelite people. The Song of Songs is read in the synagogue during the Passover holiday.

Species   A group of plants or animals that can produce offspring together. A poodle and a cocker spaniel are different breeds of dog, but they are members of the same species.

Sterilize A technique for preventing living things from reproducing. Scientists sterilize fruit flies to cut down on the number of insect pests. And pet owners sterilize ("neuter and spay") their dogs and cats to prevent new litters from being born.

Sukkot A joyous fall festival of thanksgiving for the harvest of the Land of Israel, both in ancient times and today. It also commemorates the Israelites' 40 years of wandering in the desert after the Exodus from Egypt. The decorated huts people put up for the holiday are reminders of the structures Jewish farmers built thousands of years ago during the harvests. The word *sukkot* (soo-COTE) is Hebrew for "booths," and the holiday is sometimes called the Festival of Booths or the Feast of the Tabernacles.

Sustainable harvesting A method of harvesting or using a resource so that it is not permanently damaged and not depleted. In the tropical rain forests, sustainable harvesting of resources like rubber and chocolate can yield much more economic value than cutting down trees for their lumber or burning down trees to make room for farming.

Sustainable living A lifestyle in which people consume natural resources in a careful way. They limit what they use so there can be enough for everybody in the world. They hope, too, that this way of living will provide time for the earth to replenish its resources.

T

Talmud The collection of ancient writings that explain, interpret, and broaden the teachings and laws of the Torah. The Talmud contains nearly 1,000 years of debates and discussions. This wisdom about Jewish life had previously been passed from one generation to the next only by word of mouth. But then it was written down by scholars in Israel and in Babylonia more than 1,500 years ago. The word Talmud (TAHL-muhd) comes from the Hebrew word for "learn or study."

Talons The very sharp, hooked claws of a bird of prey.

Tectonic plates The seven very large (and many smaller) shifting plates that make up the earth's surface. Each is about 50 miles thick. Usually the tectonic plates move slowly over, under, and past each other—just a few inches a year (not enough for us to feel it). But sometimes the plates get locked together until so much stress and pressure build up that one of the plates slips. The slippage is what causes an earthquake—and that's movement we do feel. As far as scientists know, Earth is the only planet in the Solar System to have plates.

Temple   The house of God that once stood in Jerusalem, as the most holy place of worship and sacrifice in ancient Israel. It was built by King Solomon in about 950 B.C.E. and is now referred to as the "First Temple." That's because four centuries later it was destroyed by the Babylonians. Rebuilt a few decades later, the "Second Temple" lasted more than 500 years until it was burned down by the Romans in 70 C.E. The Western Wall in Jerusalem is revered today because it is a remnant of the "mount" (or base) of the Second Temple.

Torah   The first five books of the Bible, also called the Five Books of Moses. In it are the origins of all Jewish laws and beliefs, as well as the ancient history and sacred traditions of the Jews. The Torah begins with God's creation of the world and ends with the death of Moses—the biblical prophet, lawgiver, and great leader of the Jewish people. The word Torah (toe-RAH) comes from the Hebrew for "instruction." It is also used as a general description of all serious writings about Jewish religion and traditions.

Tu b'Shevat   A holiday designated by the Talmud as the New Year of the Trees. It comes in early spring when almond trees bloom in Israel. Many people celebrate with a seder at which everyone sings songs and eats the fruits of trees native to Israel, such as figs, dates, oranges, almonds, and olives. In Israel, families go out to the forest to plant trees. It's a time in America when many families donate money to the Jewish National Fund. Tu b'Shevat (TOO bih-sheh-VAHT) is Hebrew for "the 15th day of the month of Shevat." That's as easy to remember as the 4th of July!

Turkey   A mostly Muslim country that sits partly in Asia and partly in Europe. It was the center of the Ottoman Empire, which ruled over Palestine and much of the Middle East until the First World War.

Tzaar baalei chaim
A Hebrew phrase (pro-nounced "tsahr bah-LAY KHIGH-eem") that means "compassion for animals." It was first used in *Sefer Hasidim* (*Book of the Pious*), written in medieval Germany. But compassion for animals was expressed long before then, beginning with the Bible's requirement that work animals must rest on the Sabbath.

Tzedakah   Charitable donations. Giving *tzedakah* is considered to be one of the most important things a

Jew can do. But *tzedakah* includes more than giving money. It also means making sure that the needs of others are met. That's why helping people is part of the Jewish holidays of Passover and Purim. *Tzedakah* (tsuh-DOCK-ah) is Hebrew for "righteousness."

Vegetarianism   A diet that eliminates meat, fish, and even products such as gelatin that are taken from animal carcasses. Vegetarians obtain the necessary protein from other food sources. A "vegan" is a vegetarian who eats only food that has grown from the earth—grains, nuts, beans, fruits, and vegetables. An "ovo-lacto" vegetarian will eat certain animal-based products, such as honey, eggs, and dairy products. Some vegetarians also choose to refrain from wearing items of animal origin—wool, leather, silk, feathers, and fur.

Windmill   An engine with freely turning blades, powered by the wind. Windmills were originally used to "mill" grains (grind them into flour) and located in buildings like the ones we still see in Holland. On farms, a modern windmill, also known as wind turbine, can be mounted on a tower to pump well water. The tall windpower machines used for generating electricity are more properly called wind generators.

Water power   *See Hydraulic power.*

World Bank   An agency started by the United States and other prosperous countries that provides loans, advice, and technical help to less wealthy countries. The World Bank was created at the end of the Second World War largely to aid in rebuilding Europe and Japan. Its mission today is to reduce poverty by promoting growth and creating jobs.

Yiddish   The everyday language once spoken by most European Jews—people referred to as Ashkenazim. Yiddish grew from a mixture of medieval German and Hebrew, with bits of Russian, Polish, and English. It became a completely separate language having its own rich and unique literature. Another everyday language once spoken by many Jews is called Judeo-Spanish or "Judezmo." It was used by the Sephardim—especially Jews in Turkey, the Balkans, and North Africa. Both Yiddish and Judezmo are traditionally written using the Hebrew alphabet.

Z

Zionism   The movement to build the Jewish homeland in Palestine. Jewish pioneers (*halutzim* in Hebrew) began to settle in Palestine during the late 1800s. Some created farms and cities. Others fought for political support in the League of Nations—the organization founded in 1919 that preceded the United Nations. After the Second World War and the tragedy of the Holocaust, the United Nations approved the establishment of the State of Israel, which declared its independence on May 14, 1948. Zionists all over the world continue to support the nation, and many come to live in the Land of Israel.

Thanks from the Publisher

Many people kindly answered questions about Jewish practices and about general ecology matters. The Jewish Publication Society is especially grateful to Rabbi Yitzchok Gurevitz, Rabbi Natan Levy, Noah Potter, Maggie Rufo, Rabbi Dovid Sears, and Marilyn Whitford. In addition, JPS thanks the following organizations, schools, and businesses for generously providing information and/or illustrations:

The American Society for the Prevention of
Cruelty to Animals (ASPCA)
http://www.aspca.org

Ardea
http://www.ardea.com

Bobbi Angell
http://www.bobbiangell.com

Bureau of Reclamation,
Lower Colorado Region
U.S. Department of the Interior
http://www.usbr.gov/lc

Central Park Conservancy
http://www.centralparknyc.org

Epona Equine
http://eponaequine.com

Germantown Friends School
http://www.germantownfriends.org

The Green Agency
http://www.thegreenagency.com

The Hungry Owl Project
http://www.hungryowl.org

Israel Images
http://www.israelimages.com

Israel Ministry of Tourism
http://www.goisrael.com

Jackson Elementary School
Everett, Washington

The Jane Goodall Institute
http://www.janegoodall.org

Jewish National Fund
http://www.jnf.org

Jungle Photos
www.junglephotos.com

keeweechic
http://members.virtualtourist.com/m/130fa

Marin Conservation Corps
http://www.marincc.org

National Oceanic & Atmospheric
Administration
U.S. Department of Commerce
www.noaa.gov

National Park Service
U.S. Department of the Interior
http://www.nps.gov

National Renewable Energy Laboratory
http://www.nrel.gov

Portland Streetcar Company
http://www.portlandstreetcar.org

U.S. Fish & Wildlife Service
U.S. Department of the Interior
http://www.fws.gov

U.S. Geological Survey
U.S. Department of the Interior
http://www.usgs.gov

Index

Boldface **page numbers** indicate chapter 12, Mini-encyclopedia.

About the Author

Chaya M. Burstein is the author-illustrator of many children's and young people's books. Two of the books have won the National Jewish Book Award. She writes about herself: "I was brought up in Brooklyn with Bible stories and shtetl stories rather than Mother Goose tales. When I grew older and joined a Zionist scouting organization, the stories I knew from childhoood were overlaid with nature lore, the experiences of overnight hikes, and love of the outdoors. I live in Israel now, on a mountaintop, in a house surrounded by a forest of tough little oak trees, which is alive with porcupines, foxes, jackals, and even wild pigs. I teach English to immigrant Jewish kids and Bedouin Arab kids, garden, write, and draw. It's a happy mixture of closeness to nature, Judaism and Israeli-ness."